MIND OF THE DEMON

A MEMOIR OF MOTOCROSS, MADNESS, AND THE METAL MULISHA

LARRY LINKOGLE

WITH JOE LAYDEN

RUNNING PRESS
PHILADELPHIA · LONDON

Books published by Running Press are available at special discounts for bulk
purchases in the United States by corporations, institutions, and other organizations.
For more information, please contact the Special Markets Department at the Perseus
Books Group, 2300 Chestnut Street, Suite 200, Philadelphia, PA 19103, or call
(800) 810-4145, ext. 5000, or e-mail special.markets@perseusbooks.com.

ISBN 978-0-7624-4766-4

Library of Congress Control Number: 2013936291

E-book ISBN 978-0-7624-4890-6

9 8 7 6 5 4 3 2 1
Digit on the right indicates the number of this printing

Design by Joshua McDonnell
Edited by Geoffrey Stone
Typography: Bembo and Print

Running Press Book Publishers
2300 Chestnut Street
Philadelphia, PA 19103-4371

Visit us on the web!
www.runningpress.com

In memory of Hunter S. Thompson

"The test of the machine is the satisfaction it gives you. If the machine produces tranquility, it's right. If it disturbs you, it's wrong."

—Robert M. Pirsig, *Zen and the Art of Motorcycle Maintenance*

"What're you rebelling against, Johnny?"

"Whaddya got?"

—The Wild One

Contents

╫╫╫

PROLOGUE

Taft, California—2004

You can get a long way from home without ever leaving the state. That's one of the thoughts whistling through my mind as we enter the shitty little ranch house on a dusty afternoon. Like a lot of folks in Taft, a once-booming oil town, we're transients, here to get a piece of the thriving local crystal meth action. We're not trafficking or anything; just using our wits and balls to collect "protection" money, and occasionally rip off the drug-addled amateurs too stoned on their own merchandise to take care of business.

There's low-hanging fruit out here, for sure, but it's also the Wild West, which is why my buddy Stan and I are on the premises, checking out the stock of a local arms dealer. I'm borderline crazy at this time, my brain muddled from all the injuries and the painkillers and the meth, so the insanity of sifting through weapons in the back bedroom of some guy's house barely registers as abnormal. And it sure doesn't seem to bother Stan, a professional mixed martial artist who is just about the craziest guy I've ever met. Even sober, Stan is a formidable presence—a little over six feet tall, two hundred pounds of muscle, and a psychotic stare. Toss in some meth and you have a man who would scare the crap out of even the most hardened drug dealer.

We're ten minutes into checking out the merchandise when a bunch of Chicano gangbangers come flying into the house. One of them, the biggest one, is covered with tattoos, including the number "805" splattered across his face. He's brandishing a steak knife and screaming at the top of his lungs.

"Where's Stan?! I gotta talk to Stan!"

This dude in the back bedroom has just shown me a .44 Magnum, so when I hear the commotion I pick it up, stick it in my pants, and run into the front room, unsure of what I might have to do or whether I'd even be willing to do it. And now I'm looking at this guy, thinking I might have to blow him away, and the whole thing starts to feel like a dream.

Suddenly, Stan is charging past me, running at the dude with the knife, ready to take the guy down without hesitation. But the guy holds his hands up in surrender, and Stan stops in his tracks.

"Stan . . . dude. You gotta help us."

The gangbanger goes on to explain his predicament. There's a party down the street that's gotten out of hand. Something to do with rival gangs and drugs and disrespect. I don't even know. I don't want to know. But Stan is into it.

The next thing I know we're climbing into the guy's car. There's another Chicano behind the wheel. He nods appreciatively, wordlessly, as Stan and I settle into the back seat. A breeze blows through the car, aided by a sizable hole in the rear window. I can feel the handle of the .44 Magnum in my back pocket, pressing against my tailbone. My heart is racing. *What the hell am I getting myself into?*

"Dude, how many of them are there at this party?"

The gangbanger doesn't even turn around. "I don't know, man. A bunch. Why?"

"Because there's only four of us, that's why!"

Stan gives me a poke in the side. "Relax, Link. We'll be fine."

I can tell he's actually looking forward to this.

My mind is racing, but I'm not exactly thinking clearly. I don't know how long it's been since I've slept. Two or three days . . . maybe more. It occurs to me, though, in a fleeting moment of rationality and regret, that my life had taken a seriously wrong turn at some point. I was one of the best young motocross racers in the world. I pioneered the sport of freestyle motocross. I had a thriving million-dollar business with tentacles extending deep into the growing world of action sports. I had legions of young fans, sponsors, endorsements. Family and friends. And now here I am, in the backseat of a car, with a loaded .44 Magnum in my pocket, heading to a gang fight that will surely end in a very bad and bloody way. I don't want to be in this situation. I don't want any part of it. But how do I escape?

Suddenly I remember that "805" up there in the front seat is packing nothing more lethal than a steak knife.

"Hey, man," I say, as the car starts to pull away from the curb. "You guys don't need us. You just need some firepower."

"Huh?"

"Yeah, check it out. Dude back there is selling guns. Go inside and grab some."

Next thing you know, we're all back in the house, and Stan and I are basically auctioning off the dealer's guns without his consent. But what's he gonna do? We'll kick the shit out of him if he complains.

A few minutes later, "805" and his friend are on their way, armed to the teeth. Part of me feels sick about it, because I know what's going to happen. But desperate times call for desperate measures.

I just want out of it. And now I am.

Sure enough, not ten minutes pass before we hear gunfire crackling through the neighborhood. Not one or two pops, but multiple gunshots—the soundtrack of a battle raging. Then silence. And, finally, the predictable bleating of sirens. I'm standing on the sidewalk as the cops close in, my heart practically jumping out of my chest. This is my world now, and I have no idea how I got here.

CHAPTER 1

I didn't start riding motorcycles—real motorcycles, I mean—until I was almost twelve years old. But it wasn't like I drifted into it after a career in football or baseball. Truth is, team sports never appealed to me. My mom had forced me into T-ball when I was younger, but I hated it. Couldn't stand waiting around all day for my one chance at the plate. I preferred action sports, like skateboarding and bicycle motocross (BMX). I had no patience for anything else.

From the youngest age, I craved the rush of adrenaline that came with nailing a trick on my skateboard or catching air on my bike. I can't speak for everyone, of course, but I think it's a common trait among participants in action sports: the pursuit of adrenaline. Even as a little kid, I kind of liked being home alone, watching a scary movie with my sweatshirt or pajamas pulled up over my face, peeking out through a corner, testing the boundaries of my bravery and fear. In some weird sort of way, I liked getting freaked out that a monster might be lurking in my closet. I embraced the anxiety . . . the unknown—I couldn't get enough of it.

Technically speaking, I grew up in Southern California, but "home" was an elusive concept. I have a great relationship with my folks these days, but childhood was something else entirely. We were a dysfunctional family. My mother, Dorian Linkogle, worked long hours and frequently traveled on business, sometimes taking up residence in far-flung cities around the country for weeks or even months on end. And Dad . . . well, he was a man with demons of his own. Les Linkogle was a Vietnam vet who suffered from post-traumatic stress disorder long before there was such a diagnosis. So I spent a lot of time home alone, or under the care of various babysitters. I remember being shuffled from one place to another: a few months with my cousins in Oregon, then a few months with my grandparents in San Diego. For at least the first ten years of my life, I did not develop any close friendships. I simply wasn't around long enough.

I am an only child, and when you move around a lot and have no siblings, you tend to find ways to entertain yourself. It wasn't just that stick and ball sports failed to capture my attention. You can't really play baseball or football by yourself, but you can skateboard and you can ride your bike. So those were the things I naturally gravitated toward. I started riding BMX bikes right around the time I started school. Seriously—I was in first grade, maybe six years old. And my dad, the competitive guy that he was, pushed me right out onto the starting line.

"If you're gonna ride, then you might as well race," he reasoned.

My father had no connection to the sport of BMX. None whatsoever. So I'm not sure why he thought it was important for his first-grader to put on a helmet and race his bike, rather than merely ride it for fun and pleasure. I know that he and my grandfather used to race Jeeps at one time, so maybe it was just a natural thing for him. I do believe it was totally about him, and not about me. Not about his ego, per se, or trying to live vicariously through his son, but about imposing his will and belief system on me. Simply put, it was all he knew. Life, to my dad, especially in those days, was all about survival and control. So of course he wouldn't see any point in riding a bike around the neighborhood for the sheer joy of it. If you had a bike, and there was a track down the street, why wouldn't you race?

I didn't mind, though. If racing meant more time on my bike, pedaling fast, then I was all for it. And I wanted to make my father proud. We were living in Orange, California, at the time, a city that should not be confused in any way with the more genteel county whose name it shares. Not far from our home was the Orange County Racetrack, where a variety of events were held on an almost nightly basis. So, one day, Dad tossed my bike in the back of his truck and drove me to the track. I was totally stoked when we arrived. Loved the atmosphere, the smell, the perpetual purple haze that hung over the track, a by-product of all that dirt getting kicked up in the air. Even as a little guy donning racing gear for the first time, I felt right at home.

There were nerves to combat, of course. I knew nothing about the protocol of racing, so I had to just watch the other kids and follow their lead in order to fit in. We were allowed one practice run prior to the race, and I can still feel the butterflies in my stomach when thinking about straddling my little blue BMX bike, leaning up against the starting gate, waiting for it drop open so that we could begin riding. I was so nervous that when I took off, I immediately lost my balance. In my tiny six-year-old mind, I was convinced that someone—probably someone bigger, as different age groups were practicing together—had shoved me in the back or clipped my tire. In all likelihood, though, it was sim-ply a matter of being overly enthusiastic: I had probably jerked too hard on the handlebars coming out of the gate and simply lost control. Regardless, I found myself face down in the dirt in the first few seconds of the first practice run of my first race.

It totally freaked me out. But I got right up and kept going, negotiated the course with relative ease, and soon found myself back at the starting line, where my father was waiting.

"What happened?" he said.

"Somebody pushed me!" I whimpered, my face still wet with tears.

My father waved a hand dismissively. Then he offered the sort of advice that people offer when they have no idea what the hell they're talking about. This would be a recurring theme over the years, where my father and I were concerned.

"Just pedal harder next time, okay?"

And so I did.

The field was smaller this time, as were the contestants—unlike the practice run, the race included only boys my age. There were maybe a half dozen riders. I was more careful about keeping my balance in the starting gate, and when the race began, I did as instructed—pedaling like crazy from the chute to the first turn, which I reached before anyone else. I was in the lead! And there I stayed for the duration of the race, an event that covered a single lap, four turns, and ended perhaps thirty seconds after it began.

I remember the thrill of crossing the finish line first, seeing the guy waving a checkered flag above me. I remember my dad clapping and smiling, proudly pumping a fist. I remember that it felt easy, like I was better than everyone else. And I remember one of the race officials handing me a little trophy, and thinking it was pretty cool, until I saw the hardware being presented to the older winners. Those guys were getting huge trophies, tall and heavy and glistening. Mine felt inadequate by comparison, and immediately I began to question the fairness of a sport that would not treat everyone equally.

"You won," my father said. "Just be happy."

I'd spend the better part of the next three decades trying to figure out how to do exactly that.

———

I should preface this by saying how much I love my father and appreciate everything he's done for me over the years, the way he's helped me and stood by me through some seriously challenging times. I should say up front how much I admire him for working through his own issues and becoming a successful businessman, a caring husband and father, a good friend, and a person of integrity. A lesser man would have quit or succumbed. Dad and I have both come a long way. But that doesn't change the fact that our early relationship, was intense and emotional, and sometimes difficult for me to figure out.

You didn't want to cross my father. Not in those days. He could be a scary dude with a volcanic temper. I remember one time when I was a kid, some would-be gangsters were driving through our neighborhood, a little too fast for my father's taste, and he shouted at them. This was back when we lived in the city of Santa Ana, a fairly rough place with a heavy gang presence. Most people knew enough to keep their mouths shut around the gangbangers, but not Dad.

"Hey, slow it down!"

The car pulled to the side of the road; the driver, a big kid who looked to be in his late teens, got out. Three of his buddies remained in the car. The two of them stood there for a moment, the kid and my dad, just staring at each other. The kid sort of hiked up his shirt for a moment, just enough to reveal a gun poking out of the waist of his pants. If this was supposed to intimidate my father, it didn't work; in fact, it had precisely the opposite effect. Dad immediately charged at the kid, screaming, "Is that a gun!? Are you pointing a gun at me?!" and cursing as he ran. I don't know why the kid didn't reach for his weapon, but he didn't, and within a matter of seconds, my father was on him, beating the kid with his own pistol.

Is that brave or crazy? I don't know, but it was life with Les Linkogle. Maybe he had a flashback from when he was in the war. He didn't talk about that stuff much, except in the abstract. He was always saying things to me like, "If you were in the military, you wouldn't last a second!" But for the longest time he wouldn't tell me anything about his own personal experiences in battle until I was around seventeen years old, when he gradually began sharing things, telling me wild stories.

One day he showed me a photograph: it was my father receiving a medal and shaking hands with President Nixon. I asked him what the medal represented, and he just grunted. Another decade passed before he told me the story. We were hunting in Montana at the time, and out of the blue, Dad started telling me about how he was part of an elite airborne division that had been dropped behind enemy lines. My father had ambushed a group of Vietcong, slitting the throat of one soldier who turned out to be a high-ranking officer in possession of some important intelligence. He told me stories of soldiers fragging their own officers, and of the general insanity of battle.

You couldn't expect a guy like that to be sensitive and empathetic, and for the most part, he wasn't. I remember my grandmother passing away (she had brain cancer) when I was in my teens and really feeling brokenhearted by her departure. In a lot of ways, I was closer to her than I was to my own parents, and her death left a significant void.

Here's how my father tried to put it all in perspective:

"Hey, at least your grandma went out easy," he said. "She didn't even know what happened. I had to watch my friends die with blood bubbles coming out of their chests!"

For all his faults, my father was at times undeniably a shrewd and ambitious businessman. I'm still not sure exactly what he did. I know he was an executive with a bank at one time and had his hand in various other business interests. I know that he once ran for mayor of the city of Orange—there are pictures from my childhood of me standing next to him, a tiny six- or seven-year-old waving and smiling out on the campaign trail. I also know that we went from having basically nothing to having a lot of property and a five-bedroom home in Mission Viejo in fairly short order.

I don't know where the money came from. I know my dad would come and go a lot. Sometimes he was home; sometimes he wasn't. He didn't have any kind of a regular office job, that's for sure. And I know this might sound weird, but I've never asked him about it. Maybe it has something to do with the fact that I don't feel like I have the right to judge anyone or demand explanations. God knows I've been mixed up in some questionable activities in my life. Maybe my dad was, too. Maybe not. I don't press him on it. In just about every way imaginable, he's a very different man now than he was when I was growing up. I figure there's no point in opening up old wounds.

But that doesn't change the narrative. Ours was a strange and transient life. The money seemed to come and go, our standard of living rising and plummeting without warning. I don't even remember how long we lived in Mission Viejo, but in retrospect it feels like a mere snapshot.

There were odd little excursions to a yacht club near Seal Beach, where Dad and his friends would meet or drink or brainstorm over business deals while their kids would hang out on the boats. For a little while, I felt like a rich kid, or what I presumed it felt like to be a rich kid.

Then, all of a sudden, we were back in Orange, the three of us sharing a humble little two-bedroom home.

What went wrong?

I didn't ask.

I knew only that the guys at the yacht club were replaced by other friends—crusty dudes who frankly scared the shit out of me but who seemed to respect my father. And not just in a casual way, but in a fearful way, as if they owed him something. That made an impression on me, the fact that these bad-ass guys were afraid of my dad. A couple times I went to a local pub with Dad, and people would get up and move if they were sitting at his favorite table. He rarely paid for a beer.

Real or imagined, my father had that kind of tough-guy vibe going on. I could feel it; in a weird sort of way, I liked it.

But life with Dad was nothing if not unpredictable. There were times when he would just . . . snap. I don't know how else to explain it, or how else to describe it. I can recall one night, when I was no more than seven or eight years old, stalling before bedtime, refusing to go upstairs and brush my teeth and get ready for sleep. Seemingly without warning, my father got up out of his chair and began yelling at me. He was so pissed off that he ripped the entire banister down—I can still see it peeling away from its foundation like an accordion, the spindles splattering against the walls in a shower of rage.

My mother was at the top of the staircase at the time, watching all of this unfold with what I can only describe as stoicism. As my father flailed away at the staircase, Mom spoke quietly and calmly, as if almost oblivious to the chaos surrounding her.

"Larry, dear . . . why don't you go to your room now?"

I woke the next morning to the sound of construction—my father hammering away at the demolished staircase, wordlessly piecing it back together. There was no discussion about what had happened, no apology or explanation. On some level I presumed it was my fault, although I couldn't quite figure out exactly what I had done wrong.

There is another image: my father standing in front of a fireplace, tossing some of the most intimate and cherished memories of his life into the flames. Photos of army buddies, letters he had written to my mother while he was in Vietnam, and letters she had written to him. I can see my mother trying to reach into the embers and extract the charred memorabilia. I can see them both crying.

I love my parents to death; whatever pain or discomfort I might have experienced when I was a little boy, it was nothing compared to what I put them through in later years. It's been remarkable to see my dad's transformation, and the way he's turned his life around. I don't know exactly what went on behind the scenes—I'm sure my mother was deeply involved—but one day my father made a decision to get help. (This was when I was in my mid to late teens and just starting to go through some bad times of my own.) It turned out that he was among the first wave of Vietnam vets to be diagnosed with PTSD. With therapy and treatment he slowly began to change, eventually evolving into the man he is today.

For me, the transformation was at once confusing and reassuring. Over the first seven or eight years of my life, my father was mostly absent; then he was around all the time, demanding and temperamental. Then he became sort of apathetic and uncaring. I mean, he cared about me to the extent that my behavior or my athletic performances reflected upon him, making him look good or bad. But I got the distinct impression that he could not possibly have cared less about how I was feeling, or whether I was hurting on the inside.

And then, after he sought treatment, I was exposed to a completely different man, one who wanted to care for me and talk with me; a man who would gently say how sorry he was for the way he treated me as a child. Even now, as an adult, I still don't know how to take that. I still feel awkward when he gives me a hug, because I grew up without open displays of affection; I rarely heard my dad tell me he was proud of me or that he loved me. He tells me that stuff now, all the time, and it still makes me uncomfortable.

But I'm working on it.

———————

I suppose I was fortunate to have relatives who were willing to take me in when things got particularly crazy at home. When I was in third grade, I spent several months living with my aunt and uncle and cousins in Oregon. I don't know that I would describe them as a poor family, but they certainly weren't wealthy. The family owned a small farm with everyone crammed into a small single-wide trailer. They lived off what was produced at the farm, so most meals included scrambled eggs and goat's milk, along with either pinto beans or kidney beans. To this day, I still can't eat eggs, and the very thought of goat's milk makes me queasy. But I loved being there. I embraced the lifestyle, including the work (all the kids helped out around the farm). It was so different from what I knew back home in California. At least there was structure and there were friends. Instead of being alone all the time, I passed each day in the company of my cousins. Cleaning out the chicken coop was a small price to pay.

It was while in Oregon that I was introduced to dirt bikes. The whole family was really into the off-road world: dirt bikes, all-terrain vehicles, four-wheel drive trucks. One of my cousins would put me on the handlebars or the gas tank of his TrailBlazer 50, and we'd go whipping through forests and down to the coastline. I was mesmerized by the whole off-roading experience: getting trucks stuck in the mud and winching them out, riding motorcycles and dirt bikes. Sometimes they'd let me ride alone, and I couldn't believe how much fun it was. By the time I returned to California, I was totally hooked.

It's a common thing for people to ask, "Where did you grow up?" For me, it's a complicated question. I guess you could say I grew up in Orange County, but I came into my own in Oregon, hanging out with my cousins and riding dirt bikes. That's where I first started to realize who I was and what I enjoyed doing; it's where I developed some semblance of a work ethic, too. But I didn't have anything that could be accurately described as a "childhood" until I was back with my parents, and, when I was ten years old, we moved to the Temecula region. That's when I feel like life really began; for it was there that my love affair with motorcycles blossomed and began to dominate my life.

Temecula is located in Riverside County, about sixty miles northeast of San Diego, and has long been home to a thriving motocross community. The terrain—rolling hills and few trees—is perfect for riding.

Ours was a nice, new house in a nice, new neighborhood, technically located in Wildomar, California, about halfway between Temecula and Lake Elsinore. Our home was part of the first stage of heavy development that, in coming years, would transform this part of Riverside County, and Temecula, in particular, into one of the fastest growing areas of the state. Although I can imagine that preservationists were up in arms about what was happening, I felt like I'd died and gone to heaven. Again, from a very practical, economic standpoint, I don't have a clue as to how this particular change came about, whether it was largely attributable to my mother's rising career with Aetna Insurance or whether my father had hit pay dirt with one of his business ventures. All I knew was that we were living in a comfortable home in a brand-new subdivision. Say what you want about the sterility of suburbia; to a kid who had been bouncing all over the West Coast, living in a state of perpetual unease, the cul-de-sac was mighty appealing.

We had neighbors.

We had friends.

Aside from my time in Oregon, I'd never really known what it was like to be surrounded by other kids. School didn't count, of course. I hated school, never felt comfortable there. I'm talking about throwing open the door in the afternoon, walking down the street, and finding a friend in every driveway. That's what Wildomar and Temecula seemed like to me.

Best of all, for a kid who loved riding bicycles, was the fact that even after we moved in, development continued unabated. The ongoing construction provided innumerable opportunities for an adventurous kid with a BMX bike. My friends and I would get together practically every day, riding and racing, working on tricks and jumps, and generally just having a lot of fun. We'd ride through the skeletal frames of houses as they were going up; we'd soar off the mountains of dirt that had been pushed aside to make room for new foundations. The whole neighborhood was like one giant playground or skate park.

In every playground, though, there is at least one bully; one kid who tries to make life miserable for everyone else.

For us, that kid was Gilbert.

His family lived at the edge of the subdivision, on a big double lot where the construction ended and the grassland began. By the time our family moved into the neighborhood, Gilbert had already acquired a reputation of almost mythic proportions. He was a giant . . . a monster . . . a kid who would kick the shit out of you if so much as thought about riding across his lawn.

Or so I was told.

"Dude, that's Gilbert's land," one of my friends told me one day, as I steered my bike toward a particularly enticing cluster of oak trees and olive trees just beyond the manicured stretch of grass that clearly belonged to someone. There were maybe a half dozen of us out riding that day. As usual, I was the new kid, and thus completely uninformed about the unofficial rules of the neighborhood. "Stay out of there!"

"Why?"

My friend shook his head, wide-eyed, like I was the dumbest kid he'd ever met.

"Because Gilbert's crazy. He'll kill you if you go near his property."

"Oh, come on," I said. "Those are some sick trees there. We can make a bad-ass fort."

"But . . . but . . . Gilbert," my friend stammered, his voice reflecting the sort of fear usually reserved for sharks and wolves and other king predators.

"Screw Gilbert," I said. And with that I raced across the street and up onto Gilbert's lawn. The others followed. We hopped off our bikes and began playing under the trees.

"See," I said. "You guys are all a bunch of chick—"

"Gilbert!" someone yelled. "Run for it!"

I swear he must have been sitting in his house, staring out the front window, serving as sentry for the family. What he was trying to protect, I have no idea. But suddenly there he was, in all his terrifying glory, pedaling his little dirt bike down the driveway and out onto the street.

Gilbert!

"Let's get out of here!" someone shouted, and just like that, they were gone. All of them, leaving me alone beneath an olive tree, staring down the oncoming train that was Gilbert.

He rolled right up next to me, threw down his bike, and began ripping off his shirt.

"Get off my property!" he yelled.

I just stared at him, this scrawny kid, about my size and age, standing there bare-chested, breathing heavily, his face flushed red. I don't know why, but he just looked . . . funny. Not scary or even particularly imposing. Just funny.

"Come on, dude," I said. "Take it easy. It's a cool spot for a fort."

Gilbert was unconvinced. He kept screaming and waving, ordering me to get off his property. And then he began to threaten me.

"Let's go, right now!" he shouted, his face close enough that I could see the veins popping out on his neck.

"Right now . . . what?" I asked.

"Me and you! Let's go!"

I figured there was no talking my way out of this one, and while I had no experience in fighting—none whatsoever—I got the sense that Gilbert wasn't nearly the killer that my friends had described. Anyway, what choice did I have? If my father found out that I had backed down to the neighborhood thug, he'd be disappointed, if not downright pissed.

"Okay," I said. "Let's do it."

Suddenly, Gilbert backed away. His hands, balled into little fists, suddenly fell to his side.

"Uh, no man. That's not what I meant. I don't want to fight."

"Well, what do you want?"

"I just want you to get off my property. Now get out of here!"

I shrugged. "No, dude. I'm not leaving."

We stood there for a few seconds, two little boys, neither wanting to fight, but both unwilling to turn the other cheek. Finally, Gilbert gave me a little shove in the chest. I responded by punching him in the head. Stunned, he stepped back, held a hand to his face, and started to cry.

"You hit me, man! Why did you do that?"

Good question. I had no answer, and as I watched him walk away, pushing his bike, I couldn't help but feel bad.

But here's the interesting thing about that little encounter: Gilbert never gave me any trouble again, and, in fact, we became good friends. Gilbert was the first boy in the neighborhood to trade in his BMX bike for a dirt bike. He had a little Honda XR 80 that he'd ride around the trails behind his property. Gilbert solicited my help in building a series of jumps and berms, a legitimate motocross track constructed entirely by hand. I swear I slaved on it for weeks, partly because I liked Gilbert and he was my friend, but also because I figured that if I worked hard enough, he'd have to repay me by letting me use his bike.

It was only fair, after all.

"Come on, Gilbert. My turn," I said one day after watching him ride for the better part of an hour.

"No way. My parents will get mad."

Finally, one day, he let me borrow the bike. I climbed aboard, hit the throttle, and roared toward the first little jump. Airborne, I'd never felt so free, so alive. I rode for the next half hour—I think Gilbert had to practically tackle me to get me off the bike. From that day forward, all I wanted to do was ride dirt bikes. I spent all my time at Gilbert's house, riding and working on the trails, building better and bigger jumps, designing new obstacles and challenges. I didn't tell my parents what I was doing, because I was sure they wouldn't approve. I'd leave in the afternoon on my BMX bike, like I'd always done, and come back covered in dirt and sweat. I figured if they asked, I'd just tell them we were riding regular bikes.

One day, though, my father came looking for me. He stood there on the edge of Gilbert's property for a while without me even knowing it, watching the two of us ride. When I got home that evening, Dad was waiting.

"So, Larry," he said. "Anything you want to tell me?"

"Don't think so."

"What were you doing today?"

"Nothing," I said. "Just riding."

He smiled. "Riding what?"

There was a long pause as I tried to devise an exit strategy. I'd seen my dad tear down a staircase over practically nothing; he might kill me for riding a dirt bike without permission.

"Dad . . ." I began.

"Never mind," he said. "You're into dirt bikes, huh?"

"Yeah, Dad. I love it."

He nodded. "Okay."

A few weeks later, my father went out and bought me a 1986 KX80 Kawasaki motorcycle, a budding dirt biker's dream. I had just turned eleven years old and knew exactly what I was going to do with the rest of my life.

CHAPTER 2

D ad got a bike, too—a big-ass Honda XR 500, with a headlight and everything. An impressive ride for a guy who had virtually no experience with motorcycles.

For a while we rode together practically every day. There was a big field across the street from our house that had become an unofficial motocross park; when we first moved in, there were only a few tracks, but by the time I got my bike, the area had been sculpted into a fairly neat little circuit. My father and I would go over there all the time, just the two of us, and we'd ride for hours on end. At first, it was a lot of fun. I'd been dreaming of having my own bike, and I couldn't believe that the dream had actually come true.

It's so hard to explain the feeling of exhilaration and freedom you get on a motorcycle—especially a dirt bike. In those days, I didn't consider it dangerous. I never worried about getting hurt, even though injuries and accidents are as much a part of motocross as they are a part of football and boxing and auto racing, or any of the myriad action sports. It wasn't that I felt invincible; I just didn't care. The thrill of riding more than outweighed the risks. The noise, the dirt, the speed—I loved all of it.

Dad taught me everything in the beginning. I mean, I had some rudimentary knowledge about how motorcycles worked, thanks to my time in Oregon—and my few sessions with Gilbert—but those were little bikes, and my experience was limited. The Kawasaki was a real motorcycle, albeit a relatively small one, and it took some practice to use it efficiently.

My father wasn't a bad teacher in those first few months, in part because he was having too much fun riding himself to obsess about what I was doing right and wrong, or whether I had the potential to be a competitive motocross rider. I had no goal, no plan, no interest in anything other than simply riding for fun. Dad showed me how use the clutch, how to throttle back while going through a turn. A lot of subtle stuff, really. I'm not sure how he even knew any of that shit, but he did. And simply by racing him around the field, the two of us riding in tandem, trading time in the lead, I learned a lot.

Before long, though, Dad's motorcycle obsession changed. He stopped riding and began watching, coaching, and directing. My life soon revolved around motocross, and my father's life revolved around me. Dad seemed to have a lot of time on his hands then. He stopped working quite so much, stopped traveling and disappearing for long stretches. Most of the time, he would just lay low, watch television, hang out around the house. Every so often a friend would stop by. Most of his friends seemed like nice enough guys (in the eyes of an eleven-year-old), but looking back on it now, I can say with some certainty that they were shady dudes. I mean, I know shady dudes; I've spent some time around them myself. Hell, I've *been* one. Some of these guys fell into that category.

Among the most memorable was a man named Bob who owned a place called the Bug Barn. Ostensibly, the Bug Barn was a Volkswagen repair shop (thus the name). But it had a real low-rent feel to it, with a bunch of scraggly kids hanging out all the time, some working as mechanics, others just soaking up the atmosphere. More than a few of them seemed to live at the shop; Bob would let them sleep there, maybe in exchange for labor.

I have no idea how my father hooked up with this guy. He hadn't owned a VW Bug in nearly two decades, since before he went off to Vietnam. Maybe they knew each other from those days. Regardless, Dad enjoyed driving over to the Bug Barn and shooting the breeze with Bob. More often than not, he'd drag me along—Dad took me everywhere in those days. He'd pick me up after school and sometimes we'd go straight to the field for a ride; other times we'd go to the Bug Barn.

Anyway, Bob was into motorcycles as well—claimed that he used to race professionally. I never saw any evidence of that, but we did ride together several times, and it was fairly obvious that he knew what he was doing. He taught me a few tricks, showed me some stuff you could do with the throttle when you jump, body position, things that I was able to pick up quickly and use to my advantage. He was a better rider than my father, probably a better teacher too, although I didn't really think of us having that sort of relationship. He was just a guy who rode with me.

One day, though, when I came home from school, my father was waiting.

"I talked with Bob today."

"Yeah?"

Dad nodded.

"He says you're ready for a race."

A race? I hadn't even thought about that. Several years had passed since my brief career as a BMX competitor, and while I wasn't opposed to the idea of being a competitive rider, it wasn't something I'd seriously considered. I'd only had my new bike for maybe four or five months. It was still a novelty.

"I don't know, Dad. I'm not sure I'm ready for that."

My father laughed.

"You'll be fine. Bob says you're a natural. There's a competition at Perris Raceway this Saturday. Bob will be there racing. I told him I'd bring you there."

"Umm . . . okay."

Perris Raceway was the oldest motocross track in California, and since the American version of the sport was born in Simi Valley, that automatically made it one of the oldest tracks in the country. Perris Raceway was (and still is) a legendary facility in the motocross world. And like a lot of kids, that's where I made my debut.

The track was located in the city of Perris, in Riverside County, roughly forty-five minutes from our house. Perris was a nice enough little city, but the track was located on the outskirts, in a run-down neighborhood. The facility was fenced off and skirted by barbed wire, in the hopes of discouraging vandals and thieves. Perris Raceway was set against a breathtaking backdrop of jagged mountains, the rocks and cliff walls emblazoned in spray paint with the names of motorcycle clubs from days gone by. It was, to the eyes of a pre-adolescent biker making his motocross debut, just about the coolest place on Earth.

To say I suffered from a case of the jitters would be a massive understatement. As we walked through the front gates of Perris Raceway, I was struck not only by the sheer scope of the place, but also by the swarm of activity and size of the crowd it had attracted. This was just a normal weekend of racing, and yet there seemed to be thousands of people on the grounds. There were bikes and trailers and trucks everywhere. A day of motocross racing can be that way, as it typically involves competition in multiple age groups, skill levels, and classifications—from eight-year-old novices on mini-bikes all the way up to adult professionals on 500 cc motorcycles, and everything in between. It's a long and very full day with hours of standing around and watching, fidgeting nervously, killing time. The boredom is punctuated spectacularly by a few minutes of racing.

As was the case with my first BMX event, I was basically clueless about protocol, so I tried to watch and listen and learn. The race would be roughly six to eight laps, maybe fifteen minutes in duration. Long enough to get seriously fatigued and beat up, but also a distance that would be forgiving of any minor errors or miscalculations—an important consideration for a neophyte. Theoretically, I could screw up on the first lap and still have time to get back in the race, which was a comforting notion.

A prerace practice run—just a couple laps—did little to mitigate my anxiety. I was so nervous that I could barely sit still. I realized then that the worst part about racing was the waiting—the anticipation. And since I had no experience with it, I erred on the side of caution. My biggest fear was that I'd be late for the start of the race, or that I wouldn't hear the track announcer when he summoned my age group and skill level (novice) and classification (80 cc) to the staging area. So I hung out in the vicinity all morning, and when I knew they were getting close, I went to the staging area. Most riders wait until the last minute; I was there at least three races ahead of schedule. Also, unlike most of the other riders, I stayed in my gear after the practice run; not just some of the gear but almost all of it: boots, chest plate, heavy-duty riding pants, kidney belt, knee pads—pretty much everything except the helmet. Only later did I discover that riders usually wait until roughly thirty minutes before a race to gear up. Otherwise, they risk hyperthermia, dehydration, and exhaustion, not to mention a somewhat less dangerous but equally problematic condition: an inability to answer nature's call in a timely fashion.

That one I learned the hard way.

By the time I got to the starting gate for my race, I was drenched in sweat and nearly exhausted. My heart was racing. Worst of all was the sudden realization that my bladder was utterly full. There I was, an eleven-year-old boy about to race a motorcycle for the very first time, and all I could think about was the fact that I had to pee in the worst way. Races went off in fairly short order, one after another, with just a couple minutes in between starts, so at any given time there were multiple races on the course. Once you moved from the staging area to the starting gate, you had to be ready to roll. There was no turning back. Certainly there was no time for a bathroom break. Since this was my first race, I knew nothing about procedure, but when the starter stepped out onto the course, in front of the gate, I knew it was time to go.

In more ways than one.

What was I going to do?

"Umm, excuse me, sir? Can you ask everyone to wait for a few minutes? I have to use the bathroom."

Uh-uh. The embarrassment of missing a race for that reason would have been worse than the alternatives. They wouldn't wait for a kid's bathroom break, so I had two choices: hold it in and hope my kidneys didn't explode going over a jump; or simply void in my pants.

I chose the latter option.

I've never told anyone that story before, but it's absolutely true. As I straddled my Kawasaki, revving the engine and waiting for the gate to drop, I pissed my pants. Just let it flow into my uniform and shook a leg to distribute the mess. The urine didn't even have a chance to cool before the starter waved his hand and yelled, "Race time, boys!" Then the gate opened, and I hit the throttle.

I don't remember exactly how many riders were in that race—roughly a dozen I would say. Enough to make it interesting. Enough to make me realize right away that motocross was a contact sport. It wasn't just about speed and timing; it was about guts and stamina and physical strength. Later I would come to understand the importance of technology—probably the single most important component to success—but here, riding against a bunch of eleven-year-old boys, skill mattered most. And skill was mainly about having balls. You opened the throttle and rode as fast as you possibly could.

I wasn't the first rider to the corner, but I was close enough that I easily closed the gap after the first few jumps. By the end of the first two-minute lap, I was in the lead. And I stayed there until we crossed the finish line. I remember that it felt both exhilarating and fairly easy, as though everyone who was in front of me on that first lap was going really slow—slower than I usually rode when I was just practicing for fun with Dad and Bug Barn Bob. So I went by them. And then a funny thing happened: I started going after some of the intermediate riders who were on the track at the same time. And I caught some of them. It's strange, because I've never considered myself a particularly competitive guy in the usual sense of the word. I was later drawn to freestyle motocross because it wasn't about competition; it was about artistry and camaraderie and adventure; it was about showmanship and creativity. But at that age, in my first race?

Oh, yeah . . . I wanted to win in the worst way. I wanted to be the best motocross rider I could possibly be.

After the race my father was absolutely ecstatic. I remember him shouting and smiling and patting me on the back. I actually tried to keep my distance from him because I was afraid if he got too close he'd get a whiff of stale piss and wonder what the hell had happened. But everyone stunk—a combination of sweat and dirt and gasoline. A little urine on top of that was barely notice-able. Unfortunately, I had another race later in the afternoon, so I had to spend several more hours just hanging out, wet and uncomfortable, letting a nasty rash develop on my legs and butt. I wasn't even nervous before the start of the sec-ond race, because the first one had been so much fun, and so uncompetitive. I knew that I was the best rider in the novice group, so I did exactly what I had done in the first race: I went to the lead and then spent most of the race trying to chase the intermediate riders. By the time we left that day, I was already thinking about how I would get to the next level.

My father was stoked too. He wanted to have his picture taken with me while I stood next to the bike, holding my first-place trophy. On the ride home he didn't stop talking about how well I'd done and how proud he was. This sort of behavior—upbeat, talkative, happy—was not something I usually saw out of him. But I liked it, and I wanted it to continue. I wanted to do whatever I could to make my dad happy. I mean, I did it for me too. I loved riding, and I was amped about winning. But the fact that my father seemed to derive such pleas-ure from it made the victory even sweeter.

We became a motocross family, with the rhythm of daily life dictated largely by my budding amateur career. While that might sound somewhat perverse, it's really not all that unusual at the higher levels of any sport. Kids train like crazy and parents work hard to pay for the mountain of expenses for coaching, equipment, and travel. We saved on the coaching because my father filled that role. But money was tight, and my mother helped defray some of the costs by volunteering to work at Perris Raceway, which gave us a break on entry fees.

For a while it was all good. Dad would really push me, and that made me a better rider. I began training and competing with older and more experienced athletes, and I started making lots of friends within the motocross community. I had other friends, too, kids who rode but did not compete, and who simply enjoyed the speed and excitement of being on a bike—an attitude that eventually I would come to embrace wholeheartedly. In those middle school years, though, I was like any other aspiring elite athlete: single-minded, driven, eager to please those who were guiding my career.

I rode every day, without fail, and without complaint, usually in the same little field behind our house. It became quite a hot spot after a while, where other riders of varying levels of ability and ambition would gather. I gravitated to the older riders, some of whom were professionals, and virtually all of whom were willing to share tricks and tips. I felt like I was part of a community, and I liked that feeling. Sure, there were sacrifices. My dad would sometimes work on my bike in the garage, tuning it up and making sure it would run smoothly. On those days he would urge me to go out and ride my BMX bike to maintain a suitable level of fitness. It wasn't something I was particularly interested in doing, but it seemed like a small price to pay.

With each step—from novice to intermediate to expert—the stakes increased. Instead of riding at Perris Raceway, we began traveling to competitions, first in other parts of California, and eventually all over the country: regional and national events in Oklahoma, Nevada, Tennessee. We were on the amateur motocross circuit. Our lives were determined by the schedule of a pubescent boy. We did this almost every weekend, my dad and I rising before the sun, loading up the truck with my bike and other gear, and driving for eight, ten, twelve hours at a stretch. My mother did not make many of these trips. She was too busy working, trying to earn the money to pay for them.

One day while working out at Perris Raceway, we caught a huge break. A Hollywood talent agent and video crew had shown up to scout for kids who might be interested and capable of taking part in a new television commercial for Honda. Scores of kids were riding around the track that day, and the guy in charge asked each of us to do a little riding and then say a few lines into a camera. I didn't expect anything to come of the "audition," such as it was. That night, however, my parents got a phone call from a representative of the production company overseeing the commercial. I'd been one of the kids selected to appear in the commercial—if I was interested.

"Hell, yeah, I'm interested!"

I thought it would be fun, and I was right. More importantly, though, it turned out to be something of a financial windfall as Honda ran the commercial for quite a long time. It wasn't life-changing money or anything, but it did help ease the burden of my racing career on my parents. There weren't a lot of sponsorships back then, especially for amateurs—you might get some equipment once in a while, but that was about it—so the additional income was a significant benefit. Residuals from that commercial allowed my parents to pay off some debt (accrued in part because they were spending so much money on motocross), and also helped finance a couple new bikes and a late-model motocross box van so that we could travel the circuit in style and comfort. A big, gas-guzzling box van might seem like an extravagance, but it's really not; for anyone who is serious about the sport, it's a necessity, allowing for the transportation of gear and crew, as well as providing a place to sleep and eat without having to pay for a hotel room every weekend. It's really the only practical way to go about the business of racing beyond the local level.

In 1989, my first full year on the amateur circuit, I competed in dozens of events, some local and regional, and some national (and even international). Among the oldest and most intense was the World Mini Grand Prix in Las Vegas, a premier event for many of the best amateur riders from around the world. If you placed in the top five at the World Mini Grand Prix, you could reasonably call yourself one of the sport's most accomplished amateurs. That was my goal; it was our family's goal.

The World Mini Grand Prix was like nothing I had ever seen before. For me, still a relative newcomer and only twelve years of age, it was overwhelming—like a high school baseball player suddenly showing up to pitch at Anaheim Stadium. A sea of banners and trucks and vans and motorcycles; thousands of competitors and spectators. I'd like to say it was a memorable event, and that my performance lived up to the setting and the expectations that I had established for myself, but it didn't work out that way. I remember being on the starting line, nervous but confident, waiting for the race to begin. I vaguely recall the gate dropping open and jostling for position as we roared toward the first turn.

And then I remember waking up in an ambulance, with my mother and father leaning over me.

"What happened?" I asked.

"You had an accident, Larry."

Mom looked like she'd been crying; dad looked concerned but also disappointed. I can't say I blamed him. We'd spent a lot of time preparing for this event, and a lot of money to get there, and I'd managed to crash and get knocked out. It wasn't anything serious, just a typical fall and a mild concussion. I recovered quickly, but the whole experience made me somewhat uncomfortable. I realized then just how important my riding had become to our family. If everyone was going to make sacrifices for my motocross career, then I damn well had a responsibility to come through for them. On this day, at least, I had failed miserably.

Over the course of the next couple of years I became a wildly unpredictable rider; I think I was probably as talented as anyone in my age group, and sometimes I would ride in a manner that reflected that ability. In 1990, for example, I redeemed myself by finishing first in my division at the World Mini Grand Prix. Other times, though, I would blow up spectacularly, failing to even place against lesser competition. It's hard to explain exactly what was going through my head in those days. I felt tremendous pressure every time I got on a bike; I didn't want to disappoint my father, and he was, to say the least, easily disappointed. Anything less than a victory was deemed insufficient.

I still loved riding; it was racing that I came to detest. Practice, too. By the time I got into my mid-teens, I hated practicing—all the running and weight lifting and repetition. I'd spend four hours mastering a single turn, and all the while my dad would be standing at the edge of the track, stopwatch in hand, shouting, "Accelerate, goddammit! Accelerate!" The reward for me was when we were finished practicing and I could call up some friends and just ride. No clock, no coach, no pressure.

The weight of expectations was more than I could handle. It was almost like my dad figured he'd put all this time into my athletic career, so there had to be some sort of payoff—and that payoff was seeing his son at the top of the podium. There were no excuses allowed. It didn't matter if I fell or got off to a bad start. If I didn't win, or at least finish in the top three, my father didn't even want to talk to me. It was that bad.

I remember once slipping on the first lap and quickly finding myself in fortieth place. I worked my ass off to climb through the pack and eventually crossed the finish line in eighth, which I thought was pretty respectable under the circumstances. Dad was waiting for me when I walked off the track, his voice dripping with disgust.

"We worked on starts all week! How did you blow it like that?"

This kind of thing happened all the time, my father flipping out after races, throwing things around, and generally acting like the Bob Knight of motocross.

"Find your own way home!" he'd shout. And then he'd drive off, leaving me sitting there all alone, stranded among a bunch of older riders, most of whom I didn't even know. Seriously, this happened on multiple occasions.

Eventually a pattern of self-sabotage began to emerge. I would actually choose not to do well at certain events simply because I was upset about something. It didn't take much to set me off: poor track conditions, an equipment problem, the slightest little injury. This was a particularly troubling issue, since motocross is obviously a physical sport and injuries are a significant and accepted part of the game. Like everyone else, I had suffered countless sprains and strains, and a few broken bones, by the time I was fourteen or fifteen years old. Every rider accepts this as a price for competing in the sport they love. But I didn't love it anymore, so I reached for anything that gave me an excuse to lose, or even to opt out entirely. Early in my career, if I got off to a bad start, I'd just ride like hell to catch up. Nothing could stop me. But now? If things didn't go absolutely perfect, I'd say, "Fuck it," and just not even try. A poor start was inevitably just the beginning of a half-assed performance that would leave me feeling shitty about myself and my father enraged.

I guess you'd say I was a head case—the kind of rider whose attitude never matched his athletic ability; who could perform up to his potential only if everything was in place—physically, mentally, emotionally.

That didn't happen often.

Right or wrong, I blamed most of this on my parents, and I came to resent them for it. I hate to say this, but it got to the point where I didn't even want to race; and when I did race, I didn't want my parents there watching me. I understand how that probably sounds—like I was an ungrateful, spoiled kid. My mother had sacrificed so much of her time and income for me. My father had sacrificed as well. He had put my motocross ahead of everything, and maybe I should have been more appreciative of that fact. But it all seemed too important; I couldn't handle the pressure and the responsibility and the expectations. I had started riding purely for the fun of it, and my dad had gotten a bike for that reason as well. What started as a hobby quickly morphed into a job—by the age of fifteen I had left the amateur ranks and turned professional—and my father was like the boss from hell.

Eventually, this had the effect of crushing my spirit and self-esteem. It made me feel low and unworthy. And eventually it just made me angry.

_____

School, as you might imagine, was not exactly a priority for me. By tenth grade I was regularly cutting classes or skipping school entirely. About the only class I enjoyed was wood shop; ironically, this was the class that proved to be my undoing.

I rarely screwed around in wood shop, because it was a class I actually liked; I wanted to be there, and I was pretty good at it. The only down side was the fact that one of my classmates was a kid I couldn't stand. His name was Kenny, but we called him "Ratboy" because he looked like a rat. He was always picking on me, always messing with me, trying to make me mad or goad me into a fight. One day around Christmastime, we were cutting out reindeer on the band saw. There were probably close to twenty of us in the class, all doing the same project, all taking turns using the saw. And old Kenny, he violated protocol by cutting in line ahead of me.

Ratboy . . . you little fucker!

I was so pissed that I started messing with Kenny. The band saw was a huge piece of equipment that ran pretty much nonstop, but you could moderate it with the use of a foot brake, although not everyone knew that. Well, when

Kenny started cutting out his reindeer, I hit the brake, which confused the hell out of poor Ratboy.

"What the hell is wrong with this thing? It's broken or something."

I let up on the brake, and the saw whirred to life. Kenny looked confused, but he went back to cutting his reindeer.

And so it went for the next few minutes. I played with the pedal, starting and stopping the band saw, butchering Ratboy's reindeer. No one really seemed to care. This was wood shop after all, and it was basically a self-paced environment. The kids who wanted to work could do so; those who didn't feel like working would hang out in a corner of the room and try to sneak a cigarette. I'm not even sure what had become of the teacher—I know he wasn't in the room when I hit the brake again and Kenny's reindeer got jammed.

"Goddammit!" Kenny yelled, as he looked at me and finally realized what was happening. "Knock it off, Larry!"

I released the brake just as Kenny tried to yank the reindeer free, causing the saw to spit it into the air. Kenny's hand, meanwhile, kept going and was sucked right into the blade. The next thing I knew, Kenny was screaming at the top of his lungs.

"My finger! Larry cut off my fucking finger!"

At first I didn't realize how badly he was hurt. I laughed at him and told him to stop acting like such a baby. Then I saw the trail of blood . . .

Uh-oh.

As it turned out, Ratboy lost only the tip of his pinky. I got expelled for it, although I didn't tell my parents for almost a month. I'd just hang out at a friend's house every day and then come home at the usual time. It wasn't until we got a subpoena in the mail saying the injured kid's parents were suing us that my parents discovered the truth.

"Uh . . . I can explain, Dad. Really."

Surprisingly—given our tumultuous relationship and my sketchy academic record—my father took my side on this one. He fought the expulsion and threatened legal action against the school for failing to provide appropriate adult supervision. In the end, I was reinstated and the lawsuit went away. The school recommended a continuation program (for students deemed to be "at risk"), and I went for a little while before dropping out entirely. I don't recall my parents getting all that upset about it, probably because it was so obvious that school wasn't right for me and because I had the potential to make some decent money as a professional rider anyway. If there was a viable career path for their wayward son, that seemed to be it. Whether I wanted it or not was almost beside the point.

CHAPTER 3

I ran with an older crowd—street kids, really, most in their late teens, early twenties. Although some of them rode bikes and surfed and skated, they weren't athletes. They liked to smoke cigarettes and drink and do drugs. I didn't do any of that stuff at the time, but I hung out with them. For the longest time, I was actually anti-drugs and alcohol. I didn't have my first beer until I was maybe sixteen or seventeen years old. Didn't smoke weed either. And no one really pressured me into it (probably because I was so much younger). It was partly about being an athlete. I used to see what drinking would do to my friends and how stupid they would get, and how sick they would be the next morning, and I just couldn't understand the appeal. I'd hear them moaning and groaning, and I'd be like, "Hey, Dude. I'm going to the gym; see you later."

But there were other aspects of the street-surf-skate life I found appealing—the "I don't give a shit attitude," mainly. I might have been sober, but I'd still go out and get in a lot of mischief; I didn't need drugs or alcohol to fuel my rage. Whatever stupid, destructive shit the guys decided to do on a given night—jump in the back of a pickup truck with baseball bats and drive down the road taking out mailboxes—I'd be right there. So basically I straddled different worlds: biker-thug friends on one side, straight-laced professional motocross colleagues on the other.

As much as I liked riding and racing—at least without the pressure—I felt much more at home with my buddies. You'd think motocross would be something of a meritocracy: ride fast, earn prize money and recognition. But it didn't always work that way. It was more about kissing ass and behaving appropriately in order to attract sponsors and get the best equipment and gear. It was a corporate atmosphere, complete with rules regarding proper attitude and attire. Come on, dudes, we're riding dirt bikes! It's not NASCAR. But that was the image they wanted to project. For me, it was too constricting, too much of a job. I wanted to have fun. I was a kid.

That was the problem. I wasn't *really* a kid anymore. I was a professional motocross rider and one of the youngest on the circuit. And as with any professional sport, you can't hope to be successful without putting in a lot of work. I had talent, but talent can take you only so far. I had neither the ambition nor the attitude required to be a motocross champion. It would take some time to figure that out.

Our family moved to the city of Temecula shortly after I dropped out of school. My father got a deal on a forty-acre estate that had fallen somewhat into disrepair. It had been owned by a man named Beldon Fields, an artisan who had once worked for the Walt Disney Corporation and who helped design and build the Fantasyland and Toon Town attractions at the original Disneyland theme park. The Fields estate in Temecula included several replicas of Snow White's cottage that Beldon had built for his wife. As the story goes, my parents got a good price on the estate, in part, because they agreed to maintain the architectural integrity of the cottages. Their real interest in the land, however, stemmed from Dad's commitment to my riding career.

In the late 1990s, my father got caught up in Temecula Valley's burgeoning wine industry and began growing grapes on the property, which he then sold to local wineries. By 2002, he and my mother decided to open their own business. It took them five years, but in 2007, the Briar Rose Winery opened, and today it is considered one of the finest boutique vineyards in the region.

But in the early 1990s, when we moved to Temecula, owning a winery could not have been farther from my father's mind. He was fully committed to providing his son with the support and resources needed to become a top-flight professional motocross racer. So he bought a huge tract of land and bulldozed a motocross course right there on the property. Suddenly I had a world-class training facility in my own backyard.

My interest, though, ebbed and flowed. Yeah, being a professional motocross racer was preferable to being a high school student, but I was never much for serious training or practice, and that didn't change when we became residents of Temecula, despite the fact that suddenly I was surrounded by some of the top riders in the world. Strategically speaking, my father had the right idea: move to a motocross hotbed, train with the best riders, and slowly ascend the ranks. Again, though, there was just one problem.

He wanted it more than I did.

I rode every day for hours on end. My father would take me to the gym to lift weights. Sometimes he'd work out right alongside me. Some days I'd hop on a ten-speed road bike and put in at least an hour of cardio work. From a training standpoint, my father knew his shit. Had I been a different person, a more eager student (and had he been a little less zealous), it might all have turned out differently. By the time we reached Temecula, though, I'd already grown weary of the routine. It was only a matter of time before our partnership would reach the breaking point.

For a while my social life in Temecula revolved exclusively around motocross—training with older, more experienced riders, and hanging out with my old buddies from Lake Elsinore and Wildomar, many of whom were also into motocross (although at a lower level). It was a fairly cloistered existence. I'll admit to enjoying the notoriety that came with being something of a prodigy, but I lacked the drive and focus to become an elite rider on the national level.

Whatever contempt I might have developed toward the sport of motocross (and it was considerable by the end), I'll admit that the guys who win national titles are serious athletes. They work their asses off, just as much as anyone who reaches the top of any other sport. If you were to talk with my father, I'm sure he'd say I had the potential to be one of those riders. He's probably right. But the window closes quickly; you're only a prodigy for so long. By the time I got to Temecula, I was nearly seventeen years old, no longer the youngest guy on the circuit, and pretty soon other young kids were passing me by.

And I didn't really care.

There was, I would soon learn, much more to life than motocross.

━━━━━━

His name was Nerdboy—or at least that's what everyone called him. He was a couple years younger than me but lived in our neighborhood and seemed to know everyone in town. Why Nerdboy? Because he was younger, smaller, a little awkward, and worked so hard to fit in with different social circles. But he was a nice enough kid and everyone liked him. So it was an affectionate nickname. Through Nerdboy I began to develop a social life beyond the motocross course. Although he would eventually get a bike and take up riding on a purely recreational basis, he was a stranger to the sport when I met him, and so our friendship revolved around other, more traditional adolescent pursuits.

It wasn't unusual for me to pick up Nerdboy after school. He was fifteen and couldn't drive, so he'd sometimes call me in the morning, or during the school day, and ask me to swing by in the afternoon. Then we'd hang out for a while. Well, one day I rolled on down to school and there was Nerdboy waiting outside with some chick.

"Hey, Link," he said. "This is Hannah. You mind giving her a ride home?"

"No problem. Hop in."

Hannah lived in a very upscale neighborhood; it was clear her parents had some serious cash, and that Hannah led a privileged life, as did her older sister, Paige, who was hanging out at home when we arrived. Like me, Paige was seventeen. Unlike me, she was still in school (she was a senior), although she looked more like a delinquent than I did. Not that there was anything wrong with that. I could tell right away, just by looking at her, that Paige was a gnarly chick: smokin' hot, with dirty-blond hair, angular features, tight clothes, and a way of carrying herself that could put a guy back on his heels.

"Little old to be driving my sister around, aren't you?" she said through a crooked smile.

"Uhhhh, I'm just giving her a ride home," I stammered. "No big deal."

Paige laughed.

"Yeah, I know. Relax, okay?"

She gave me a hard look. I was incredibly nervous. I had little experience with girls at this time, and Paige was out of my league in so many ways: she was rich, gorgeous, and clearly aggressive.

"We should hang out some time," she said.

I shrugged my shoulders. "Yeah, that would be cool."

And so we did. Paige was my introduction to the world of sex, drugs, and rock 'n' roll. God, I loved her. And by that, I mean I was absolutely obsessed with her. She was a full-on punker chick, with the plaid skirts, boots, a pierced nipple, and an infatuation with listening to music only on vinyl, even though the rest of the world had already buried its cassettes and moved on to compact discs. She chain-smoked cigarettes and chewed gum incessantly to kill the taste. There was a touch of gravel in her voice—probably not so attractive in later years, but in a gorgeous seventeen-year-old, it only added to the allure.

Since I was basically living like an adult anyway and making some money (although not much) as a professional rider, my parents had given me permission to live in one of the guest cottages on our property. My life was almost completely owned by motocross, so I don't think they worried all that much.

Until Paige came along.

My first girlfriend, she was deep into a lifestyle that I never even knew existed. I wasn't just innocent, I was oblivious. But that all changed pretty quickly. With Paige (and Nerdboy) as my guides, I nurtured a social life that would have terrified my parents, had they known it was happening. I mean, they had a general idea since Paige spent vast amounts of time at my place, often staying the night, and clearly they weren't thrilled by our friendship. Just looking at Paige would have set off alarm bells for most parents (including her own!), and rightfully so. She was the queen of the party chicks in town, and I became her constant companion. One night we'd drive to some old abandoned warehouse; the next night we'd be out in the avocado groves. Paige knew everyone and everything. Her popularity transcended social barriers. She came from a straightlaced, wealthy family, which meant she had friends who were cheerleaders and honors students; but she could hang with the punks and stoners as well.

Everyone thought Paige was cool, and since I was her boyfriend, I was cool by association.

It didn't even matter that I abstained from drugs and alcohol for the most part. I figured out how to go to a party, nurse a single can of beer for hours, and just chill while everyone else smoked weed or drank themselves into a stupor. No one ever really tried to pressure me, maybe because they knew I was an athlete. More likely, they just didn't give a shit. Regardless, I met a lot of friends through Paige and the party scene, and a fair number of them remain friends (or at least acquaintances). I liked their attitude for the most part—the energy and recklessness. A lot of them were kids who were drop-outs, hadn't done well in school, or who just seemed to be pissed about one thing or another. They were punkers with the rolled-up jeans and mohawks, and I dug their rebelliousness even though I'm not sure they had any idea what they were rebelling against. Their lives were chaotic, and I was drawn to the chaos.

A typical night would consist of a party followed by some vandalism or a raid on some other party where the goal was no more ambitious than to fight and steal their kegs. It was stupid and anarchistic, and I loved it. For the first time in my life, I felt I belonged. I was an athlete—a more accomplished athlete, in fact, than the kids who were captains of the football or basketball teams—but I was never part of that clique, never played team sports or wore a letterman's jacket. The punks hated the jocks, but ironically they didn't see me as a jock.

Socially, I'd never felt like I was part of a group. I'd always been kind of a loner, immersed in the singular pursuit of motocross. Now I had friends. Crazy and self-destructive as it might have been, I had a social life, and the more I became immersed in that life, the less I wanted to ride. After so many years of leading a sheltered, narrow existence, one in which I had few friends or interests outside of motocross, I was eager for a change—and this was just about the most radical departure imaginable. That may not be a rational explanation, but it's the best I've got.

After a while, the craziness became normal. What once seemed almost unfathomable became routine, and guys I once would have described as flat-out thugs became my closest friends.

There was, for example, Uncle Dino. He was the firecracker of the whole bunch, always in trouble for one thing or another. I'd seen Uncle Dino at various parties but never really talked to him much. He was a legitimately scary dude, constantly getting in fights with friends and enemies alike. I tried to keep my distance from Uncle Dino when I first started hanging out with Paige, partly because I got the impression that he had the hots for her and therefore wasn't a big fan of mine. It wasn't the best situation, and so I tried to keep a low profile whenever Uncle Dino was in the vicinity. Unfortunately, that wasn't always possible, because Uncle Dino was not exactly the type of guy who shied away from a confrontation. He was aggressive and opinionated. If you were on Uncle Dino's shit-list for whatever reason, you could count on eventually having to deal with him; you couldn't just walk away.

One night Paige and I went to a big outdoor party, and I noticed right away it was a nastier group than usual. There were a lot of guys I didn't recognize doing some seriously heavy drinking. Supposedly, they'd just invaded a jock's party in a different neighborhood, smashed the windows in a house and stolen a keg, so everyone was still pretty amped up from that little battle. As the night wore on, fights kept breaking out among these guys. You'd see them hanging out talking, drinking, like best buddies. Then all of a sudden they'd start wrestling, and then someone would throw a punch. Pretty soon they'd be kicking the living shit out of each other. I'm talking serious street fighting, like something you'd expect from mortal enemies. But they were actually good friends. The fights would go on for a few minutes until someone was knocked out or too exhausted to continue, and then invariably they'd hug it out and go back to partying. Strangest fucking thing I'd ever seen.

Whoa . . . these guys are crazy!

In the midst of this insanity, well into the night, Old Uncle Dino made his way over to me. I'd been trying to keep a wary eye on him all night. I could tell he was watching Paige; more importantly, I could tell he was watching me. Trouble seemed inevitable.

"Hey, man," Dino said, his voice hard and deep, the look in his eye a mixture of stoned detachment and outright menace. Now, I'm not a little guy these days, about six feet one, 210 pounds. But I was a wicked late bloomer and didn't fill out until I was well into my twenties. At that time I was maybe six feet tall and 170 pounds. Dino was bigger, older, stronger, tougher—a legitimate badass. And crazy enough to act on any urge.

"What's up?" I said, trying to hide my anxiety.

Uncle Dino moved closer, until our faces were only a few inches apart. Punk and metal filled the air, so it was hard to talk without getting up close and personal, but I got the distinct impression that Dino wasn't merely trying to have a friendly chat. He was invading my personal space, and there was purpose behind his movements.

"You know those guys?" he shouted.

"What guys?"

"The jocks, man. At that house, where we got the keg."

I could feel the hair rising on the back of my neck. My stomach began to roll a bit, the butterflies taking flight just as they did before a big race, only this was much worse. Uncle Dino's actions were clearly designed to make me feel uncomfortable, and the strategy had worked. I was completely caught off guard, so I tried to take a step back with the hope of diffusing the situation without looking like a pussy.

Dino stepped right into me again.

"I heard you were friends with one of them," he said.

Now I was really nervous. Dino was drunk and pissed off; even if I had hit him in the face, I'm not sure he would have felt it. And I was no fighter. I'd grown up with a dad who suffered from PTSD-fueled bouts of rage. I'd spent my whole life trying not to piss him off. I knew how to avoid confrontation. Here it was, though, staring me right in the face.

"Look, man," I said. "I don't want any trouble."

Only it didn't come out that way, I had a bit of a stutter in those days, a condition exacerbated by nervousness. Uncle Dino laughed and came right back at me.

"Wha-Wha-Wha-What did you say?"

I took a deep breath. By now I was prepared for the inevitable ass-kicking to follow.

"I said no. I don't know any of them."

Dino put his nose close to mine, stared into my eyes, and then suddenly pulled back. He gave me a little punch in the arm and smiled.

"Okay," he said. "You want a beer?"

Jesus Christ . . .

A few seconds passed before I could formulate an answer. I felt like I had been on death row and was suddenly given an eleventh-hour reprieve.

"Uh, sure. I'll have a beer. Thanks."

By the time the party ended, Uncle Dino and one of his good friends had gotten into one of those brutal, impromptu fights. He and a buddy were dancing drunkenly, hugging, laughing, and then suddenly they were throwing punches, wrestling, apparently trying to kill each other. They very nearly succeeded. The fight ended when Dino tossed his friend into the embers of a fading campfire, and the guy came up wailing with some fairly serious burns on his face and arms. I felt bad for the guy, but mainly I just felt relieved that it wasn't me on the receiving end of Uncle Dino's outburst.

Funny thing is, Uncle Dino and I became close friends after that night. I'd run into him at parties all the time, and eventually he started coming over to my house to hang out. I became part of his crew, and the more time I spent with him, the less time I spent on my bike. I still raced, and I still rode for fun. But I had little or no interest in serious training. I became one of those guys who got by almost exclusively on God-given talent. Motocross was a sport populated mainly by followers. They were too serious, too conformist for me. Uncle Dino and Paige and all of their friends were the antithesis of what I'd known. They were cool, and I wanted to hang with them as much as possible.

Look, I don't hold anyone else accountable or responsible for the things I've done with my life, or the things I did or did not accomplish. If Paige was my conduit to the wild side, well, I went there willingly, eagerly. Same thing with Uncle Dino and everyone else who embraced the thug lifestyle. They didn't twist my arm. They didn't bribe me. They were just there—in the right place at the right time.

Mom and Dad naturally grew to hate Paige. It wasn't that she was mean or disrespectful to them; she wasn't. But they were sharp enough to recognize the influence she was having on their son. They just presumed that if I was hanging out with her, I was probably into some bad shit, which I was. Although for a while, my involvement was only peripheral. For example, Paige used to sell weed. Just tiny amounts to pick up some change here and there. Despite her family's affluence, Paige was not a spoiled little rich girl. In fact, just the opposite was true. Her parents were not the type to give her whatever she wanted, probably because she wasn't living the life they wanted her to live.

As Paige once explained, "They want me to ride horses and go to college. Fuck that!"

They tried to keep her on a short leash, and part of the strategy was to periodically withhold financial support. Paige was a clever girl, though, and she figured out that she could finance her own party chick lifestyle by selling small amounts of weed. I watched her do this and got the brilliant idea to go into business with her. At that point, I wasn't even into smoking weed, but if we could clear a grand every month just by harvesting a few plants . . . well, what was the harm in that?

Paige had gotten some seeds from a friend of ours, a guy named Tyler who had a little first-hand experience in this sort of thing. Tyler gave us a brief tutorial on how to cultivate marijuana plants indoors, and we set up shop in the attic of my guest house. In all candor, I never once assessed the moral or legal ramifications of this endeavor, never lost a moment's sleep over the risks involved. I wasn't even a drug user at the time, let alone a drug trafficker, so the weight of those terms was lost on me. I saw this as a fairly straightforward business endeavor: grow some weed, sell it to our buddies (who were, after all, going to buy weed from someone, so why not me and Paige?), and pocket some much-needed cash.

We planted the seeds, and before long we had a nice little crop—six or seven healthy plants—growing beneath halogen lights in the attic. All was good. Harvest time was near and customers were ready. And then Mom paid an unexpected visit.

I wasn't there at the time, so Mom just let herself in. Inexperienced as I was in the art of growing and selling weed, I'd left the attic door unlocked and slightly ajar. My mom saw a sliver of light from above and began tracing its source. It didn't take her long to figure out was happening. I was at Paige's house when she called.

"Oh, my God, Larry! What are you doing?"

"Umm . . . what are you talking about, Mom?"

"Don't play that game with me!" she yelled. "I'm in your apartment right now. You're growing marijuana!"

Now, my father was the angry person in our family, the one prone to wild and violent outbursts. My mother had always been calm and reserved, forgiving and supportive almost to a fault. So this outburst caught me off guard. She was completely distraught, and her anger and disappointment left me practically speechless.

"Take it easy, Mom."

"Don't you tell me to take it easy! You need to get home and get this stuff out of here. Right now! Before the cops get here and arrest everyone."

There was a pause.

"No, never mind. I'll rip it up myself!"

"Whoa . . . Mom. No. Please, don't do that. I'll take care of it."

"Now, Larry!"

She hung up the phone.

Within minutes Paige and I had driven to my house and removed the plants from my attic. We ended up giving them away to Tyler and a few friends, who happily acquired our little business venture for themselves. We never did see a dime from that one. I guess I should have known right then that I wasn't cut out for a life of drug use or trafficking.

My path to full-blown drug addiction, and the descent into hell that followed, was probably somewhat unusual. I never did become much of a drinker, and it would be a couple more years before I fell for weed. Alcohol is brutal—you almost have to admire the stamina and pain threshold required to become a full-blown alcoholic—and weed, well, like I said . . . I didn't like the idea of inhaling smoke into my lungs. Oddly enough, though, I was open to the idea of experimenting with drugs generally considered to be far more dangerous and unpredictable.

The first time I ever got really sizzled—on anything—was during this same general time frame. I was seventeen and hanging out at Tyler's house one day. Tyler's mom was a full-blown hippie, looked like she stepped out of a time machine from the late 1960s. She was a nice enough woman but could not have cared less about what went on in her house. Tyler had two little brothers, both in middle school, and they were all allowed to smoke weed in the house. I'm dead fucking serious. Everyone smoked weed over at Tyler's house. It was just a cool thing to do: hang out, listen to vinyl, get stoned. And his parents seemed to have no problem with it. I don't know, maybe they just figured it was safer to have Tyler and his brothers getting fucked up under their own roof rather than out at some party.

Anyway, one day we were all chilling out at Tyler's place when Paige pulled out a few tabs of acid.

"Come on," she said. "Trip with me."

This was new territory for me. I had heard about LSD partly because my dad was a product of the sixties and talked fairly openly, and critically, about the drug use he'd seen in Vietnam. As far as I knew, acid meant bad trips and flashbacks and possible brain damage. Generally speaking, it was best to avoid it.

"Oh, I don't know," I said, looking at the little white pills in Paige's hand. She smiled.

"It's not that bad. Trust me. You'll like it."

There was a pause. Paige, a veteran tripper, began separating the acid into doses.

"Here—I'll do three; you can do half a hit. You'll be fine."

She gave me a kiss. "I'll be right here with you."

Well . . . if you put it that way . . .

I took the acid and felt absolutely nothing. Waited about ten or fifteen minutes and still felt nothing.

"This is bullshit, man."

No sooner had the words passed my lips than I began to feel a tightness in my chest. Everything began to move in slow motion. I'm not sure exactly whose idea it was, but pretty soon we were all in a car, driving through Tyler's neighborhood stoned and tripping. It was early evening, and I remember looking out the window and seeing headlights approaching and thinking that the ground and the trees appeared suddenly to be draped in icicles.

Nothing looked real.

I began to freak out.

"Oh, God . . . What's happening?!"

There was a loud thump, and then Paige pulled her car over to the side of the road. Here we were, not more than a mile from Tyler's house, with a flat tire. No one else seemed even fazed by this development, but I totally panicked.

"We gotta get out of here!"

"Easy, Larry," Paige said. "It's no big deal."

Yes it was. Or so it seemed to me, anyway. I ran down the ice-covered street and then scrambled up an ice-covered hill, where I crouched low and waited for . . . what? I was in a state of complete paranoia. When the cops and the tow truck arrived, I watched in stunned silence as a seemingly sober Paige deftly charmed everyone.

How can she be doing that?! I can't even think straight!

The tire was changed, the cops rolled away, and I ran back down the hill where Paige and Tyler and a few others were waiting. I must have looked awful because Paige took my hand and tried to calm me down.

"Just roll with it," she said. "Enjoy the trip."

Enjoy it?! I'm losing my mind here.

We all went back to Tyler's house to ride it out in safety, but that turned out to be something of a mistake for me. I think I would have been okay if I had stayed outside. Instead, I soon found myself in Tyler's basement, watching the walls come to life, heaving and moving in great undulating waves. I could hear heavy breathing, as if the walls had giant lungs. I sank into the couch, tried to close my eyes, but the hallucination lived on.

"What the fuck, man?!" I cried.

I looked around the room, stared at all my friends. I could hear them laughing, talking, and occasionally I was aware of someone holding my hand or trying to ease my concerns. And then reality began to sink in, and I was filled with anger toward my friends, and self-loathing for what I'd done.

What am I doing here? Why am I hanging out with these people, these losers!? Why am I doing drugs?! I should be out riding. These people don't have the ambition that I have! I want to do something with my life.

This was a bad trip. A very bad trip. And it kept getting worse. Eventually Paige and Tyler and everyone else headed out to a party. I stayed behind, hoping the acid would wear off and I could go home. But the trip just intensified. I began seeing goblins and ghosts. I was scared shitless. And all alone.

And then I wasn't alone.

"Here you go, Larry. Try this."

It was Tyler's mom, handing me a mug of hot tea. She sat down on the couch beside me, threw an arm over my shoulder, and gave me a hug.

"I'm with you, honey," she said. "Don't worry."

And that's how it went, Tyler's hippie mom riding out the trip with me, talking me down, feeding me tea, and staying right by my side, until the walls stopped breathing and the ghosts and goblins faded away.

Believe it or not, Paige and I went to her senior prom together. She and a bunch of her country club friends picked me up in a limo that her parents had rented. This was Paige's other life—the one her mom and dad approved of; the one in which she dressed appropriately and hung out with other affluent, ambitious kids. They even got us a hotel suite for the night, presumably because they knew we were going to be partying, so why not party in relative safety?

But Paige was risky business. On the way to the prom, while I was talking with a classmate of hers named Dave (a good dude who later became a snowboarding buddy of mine), Paige flipped open her little white purse and dug out a handful of pills. She opened her palm to show everyone what she had.

"Here, take one of these."

As was the case when we had dropped acid, there was no introduction or warning, only a sweeping dismissal of any concern I might have.

"What is it?" I asked.

"No big deal," she said, rolling her eyes. "Just try it."

I figured it was probably Vicodin or Hydrocodone, both of which I had taken very briefly following motocross injuries. The opiate-based painkillers were really making the rounds in those days. They worked well, provided almost miraculous relief to people who suffered from chronic pain or who were recovering from surgical procedures. The addictive properties weren't yet well known, so the drug was easy to obtain and its recreational use soon became widespread. Kids would raid their parents' medicine cabinets and bring it to parties. Hydro was everywhere. I knew what it was, and I wasn't particularly worried about it. Down the road a bit I'd get into Hydro in a big way, but at this point? Not in the least. In fact, I'd never gotten high on Hydro or Vicodin. I considered it a point of pride to get through injuries with as little pain medication as possible—you know, tough guys would just grit their teeth and suffer; pussies took the pain meds.

Or so I thought. Turns out I was wrong on that one as well.

Anyway, I popped one of the little pills, figuring it wouldn't even have much of an effect. It wasn't until a short time later, when we all started tripping, that Paige revealed the truth. It wasn't Vicodin or Hydrocodone that we'd taken; it was Ecstasy.

Well, needless to say, we didn't spend a lot of time at the prom—basically just popped in and had our pictures taken and then started hallucinating and losing our marbles. Much of that night is a blur to me. I remember that we all sort of went our separate ways. Or maybe I just left everyone else. I honestly don't know. I recall going to the hotel for a little while, and then I remember wandering around the streets of downtown San Diego all by myself, hanging out with bums and pan handlers and drug addicts, totally spracked out, feeling like I wanted to jump out of my skin. In no way would you call it a "good" high. It was almost like being on a meth jag (another experience I would later come to know intimately). I was amped and stoned, but also overcome with anxiety and tension. It was horrible and in many ways even worse than the bad acid trip at Tyler's house, since it went on all night and into the next morning.

When is this ever going to end?

I returned to the hotel shortly after sun up and found a scene like something out of *Animal House*: kids passed out everywhere, some still in their formal prom attire, others wearing nothing at all. The whole room stunk of liquor and vomit. One guy was on the floor, his pants soaked with urine. Just about everyone there looked to be in worse shape than me, and I couldn't have felt worse. I took some pictures to commemorate the event then went home to sleep it off, which proved to be a much more difficult and unpleasant task than I had anticipated. One half of a single Ecstasy tablet messed me up like you wouldn't believe. I couldn't sleep, couldn't eat. A thunderous headache set in that morning and didn't relent for days.

"Never again," I said repeatedly between trips to the toilet. "Never, ever, ever again."

———

One of my closest and most fucked up friends around this time was a kid named Brian Denny. Brian's parents had both been killed in an accident when he was a child, and he was subsequently raised by his grandparents. Brian had received a substantial inheritance from his parents, which was held in trust by his grandparents until Brian reached the age of eighteen. By that time, though, his grandfather had also passed away; he, too, left Brian a huge pile of money.

Brian lived all alone in a ten-bedroom mansion in a gated community, and his house became party central, as well as a safe haven for kids from a wide range of backgrounds. There were rich kids like Paige and thugs like Uncle Dino all congregating under one roof, sometimes for days on end. If you needed a place to crash, you were welcome to hang out at Brian's house. And here's the really cool thing: his grandmother lived in a guest cottage on the property, and we'd all spend a lot of time with her. She'd come over and have dinner with us, hang out and watch television, and as her health began to decline, we'd take care of her. Gramma Denny never judged any of Brian's friends and seemed to genuinely like everyone. She was such a sweet old woman.

Eventually, though, she became ill and we began to see less of her. Whether it was coincidental or not, I don't know, but Gramma Denny's diminished presence in the house coincided with a dramatic escalation in partying. The crowd at Brian's became gnarlier; it used to be a place where kids would hang out and drink beer and smoke weed and ride bikes and have sex, but now it became a much wilder scene. Harder drugs infiltrated the house in a big way. You'd see syringes scattered about in the morning, and kids so strung out on heroin that they looked like they were dead. Frankly, this scared the shit out of me. I saw what the drugs were doing to some of my friends, how it changed their person-alities and sucked the life right out of them. Everyone draws their own line in the sand on this shit, and I drew mine here. So I spent less time at Brian's and more time riding.

That's the thing about being an addict. You can always make excuses; you can always blame someone else for your weakness. But the truth is, you do have a choice; it's making the right choice that can be challenging.

CHAPTER 4

Frustration led to outright rebellion.

I stopped caring whether I finished first or thirty-first. I neglected to properly tend to my bike—not from a mechanical standpoint, but from an aesthetic point of view. I wouldn't wash or rinse the bike before a race. I started drawing cuss words in thick black marker all over the frame. I didn't want any sponsors because when you have sponsors they make you feel like you're obligated to them, and they dictate what you can and can't do.

"Keep this up," my sponsors would say, "and we'll cut you off, Larry."

"Good, cut me off. I don't want to deal with you anymore."

Here I was, traveling the world, racing motorcycles for a living, and the only thing I enjoyed about it was pissing off the officials and doing big jumps on the track, sometimes even ramming other riders just for the sheer fun of it. On more than one occasion I cut off another rider, provoking not only a collision that took us both right out of contention, but a wild confrontation between our respective pit crews as well. I lived for that sort of thing; I thrived on anger and chaos.

The stiff collars in the mainstream motocross world hated my guts, of course, and I can't really say that I blame them. They felt like I was disrespecting their sport and threatening their livelihood—and I was.

I also did not give a fuck.

Looking back on it now, I wonder sometimes what I might have been able to accomplish as a racer had I put my heart and soul into it, had I trained to the full extent of my capabilities. My competitive peak came at the age of fifteen or sixteen. After that I was basically just a fast local pro. I never really liked super-cross; it is basically an Americanized version of motocross, designed for stadiums and arenas and television, with crowds right on top of the action. Supercross tracks are shorter than motocross tracks, the courses slower and more technical. I was more of an outdoor motocross guy, but I never had the endurance to compete with the best riders. I was good for maybe ten laps, so I could win the shorter qualifying events, but then I'd fall back into the twenties or thirties in the finals. I lacked the fitness and conditioning to ride effectively for an entire day against world-class competition. As is true at the highest level of any sport, there's no margin for error, no room for laziness. I simply didn't want it bad enough. I didn't train hard enough. So when it came time for the big show, I had nothing in me.

By the mid-1990s, when I was not yet even twenty years old, I had pretty much given up on formal training and abandoned any pretense of ambition in terms of motocross racing. Depending on your perspective, I was a knuckle-head, anarchist, or innovator.

There was no such thing as freestyle motocross at that time, but there was "free riding," and it was this aspect of the sport I enjoyed most: just getting out on my bike, hitting the trails and hills and sand dunes, covering dangerously wide gaps, coming up with impromptu tricks, like letting go of the handlebars or kicking my legs off to the side, and generally just having fun, like when I was a kid visiting my cousins in Oregon, tooling around on mini-bikes. It was sim-ple. It was pure. No pressure, no expectations, no rules or regulations.

Just me and the bike.

I wasn't the only one into free riding. Not by a long shot. It actually had become something of a movement in Southern California, expanding and growing organically from San Clemente and the other beach towns of Orange County, to the hill country of Temecula. San Clemente was a particularly tough place, populated by lots of gnarly stoners, surfers, and skaters. Some of these guys, like Christian Fletcher and Nathan Fletcher (surfing), and Trigger Gumm (skateboarding), were seriously talented athletes in their own right, but they liked to jump on a bike in their spare time and do some free riding. Hanging out with these guys confirmed what I already suspected: that I preferred free riding to competition, and partying to serious training.

The free riding movement soon took on a life of its own, its popularity and recognition boosted dramatically by the work of a couple filmmakers named Jon Freeman and Dana Nicholson. Jon and Dana spent the better part of two years gathering "behind-the-scenes" footage of professional motocross riders. With a speed metal soundtrack and endless shots of motorcycles soaring over cars and buses and trees, *The Crusty Demons of Dirt* was released by Fleshwound Films in 1995 and quickly developed a cult following.

The only problem with that first entry in the *Crusty Demons* catalogue (there would eventually be more than a dozen titles) was the fact that it featured almost exclusively athletes from the racing world. I get that—the whole point was to show these guys away from the track, having fun, and yet still be able to exploit their names in an attempt to sell some videos. That strategy had been working in the snowboarding video world for some time, so why not motocross? Nevertheless, these guys weren't really even doing anything special. In those days, it was a big deal for someone like Micky Dymond to celebrate a victory by going big off a jump after the race, or for Jeremy McGrath to briefly loosen his grip on the handlebars on the last lap of a qualifying heat, with nothing at stake. Crowds loved that shit! In all honesty, though, me and my buddies—and a ton of other riders from all over the world, as it turned out, were hitting bigger jumps and doing far crazier stuff every day, with no one watching.

Pretty soon, though, as word spread, everyone was watching. I made it into *Crusty Demons 2*, which depended less on the name recognition of familiar motocross racers than it did on the jumping ability and indomitable "I don't give a fuck" attitude of true free riders. Guys like Seth Enslow and Mike Metzger. Before long the two worlds—free riding and racing—began to overlap and intersect. Some of my buddies who knew how to ride and jump, but who had very little racing experience, would occasionally nudge their way into a formal motocross event; and like me, they rarely showed it the proper reverence, preferring instead to inject some orchestrated rowdiness into the proceedings—riding recklessly, going big on the jumps, bumping other riders—to get a rise out of the crowd.

No one thrived on this more than I did. What most racers viewed as a promotional stunt to fatten their endorsement deals, I embraced as a way of life. I continued to race, though not very effectively, preferring instead to wreak havoc on my fellow competitors while simultaneously entertaining the crowd and fueling the freestyle movement. My continued presence on the professional circuit annoyed the hell out of traditionalists in the American Motorcyclist Association, which oversees both motocross and supercross. But there wasn't much they could do about it. I mean, they could disqualify me if I did something unsafe during a race, but as long as my bike passed technical inspection, they couldn't prevent me from entering a competition. So if I wanted to shave the top of my head, let my curly hair grow out on the sides, and paint it orange like Bozo the Clown (which I did), they couldn't stop me. If I wanted to roll up to an event dressed like Elvis, complete with polyester bellbottoms and stick-on sideburns (which I did), they could only mutter under their breath in frustration. They couldn't even stop me from taking a big Sharpie pen and writing "FUCK OFF, POSERS!" on my bike, or adorning it with the most repugnant images you can imagine: bodies ripped in half or bloody corpses hanging on meat hooks.

What did I care? I had no sponsors to please, no obligations to anyone except myself, and what I considered to be the true spirit of the free rider.

Nebulous as hell, huh?

But then a strange thing began to happen. What should have been career suicide became an unexpected opportunity. Crowds had always enjoyed watching riders celebrate after victories, or hit big jumps during a race. But it was merely a sideshow. Thanks to the *Crusty Demons* videos, though, free riding came to be viewed as something that might be worth pursuing in its own right. It made underground stars out of people like me. It made us antiheros, and I kind of liked that. So, too, did a small handful of sponsors who were willing to think outside the box—especially if there was money to be found there.

SMP started out in 1989 as a small company founded in Orange County by a group of skating and surfing buddies. Their clothing and gear soon became visible throughout the action sports world, most notably among snowboarders. They had no visibility in the motocross world primarily because they were a controversial company whose name was steeped in mystery and rumor. Depending on who you asked, SMP was an acronym for "skate more parks," "surf more pipes," "snowboard more peaks," "sex money power," or any number of other possibilities. Most people, though, figured SMP stood for the obvious: "smoke more pot." That was fine with me. By this point, I'd become a big-time weed user—it was part of the free-rider lifestyle, and I was in the thick of it. More importantly, SMP seemed to love the whole idea of freestyle motocross; they saw possibility where the AMA saw only disrespect and interference. The AMA wanted to squash the very notion of free riding, or at least keep it away from their sport. And they sure as hell didn't want any of their riders being sponsored by a company that advocated getting stoned.

For a long time, SMP was totally cool with everything I did. They liked my personality and my antics—and the fact that I was a legitimate racer (although not a very good one at that point) as well as a popular free rider . . . a true

Crusty Demon! They gave me gear and a small salary. They developed a marketing plan around freestyle, and I was a big part of that plan. I couldn't have been more surprised by this arrangement, and I mainly had Brian Manley to thank for it. Brian had been a very successful motocross racer; he was fast and talented, and always seemed to have the hottest chicks. I'd really looked up to him as a kid. After retiring as a competitive rider, Brian went to work for SMP as a team manager; he scouted me, witnessed my antics, and for some reason decided to bring me on board, despite all the obvious baggage. (Nathan Fletcher also joined the SMP stable, as did Tommy Clowers, a very fast racer who eventually turned to freestyle full time.) Best of all, Brian made it clear that there would be no constraints. I could be myself. SMP would support my career and indulge my eccentricities.

And they did. At least for a while.

I use the term "career," but that's a bit misleading; I had no plan, no strategy, other than to make riding fun again, and to spit in the face of the sport that I had once loved but now loathed. If people got a kick out of watching me raise a middle finger to the whole sport, I had no problem with that.

When it became apparent that some of the folks who came out to watch supercross events actually were more entertained by some of the stunts I began to pull . . . well, that was interesting. Then I realized there might be some greater force at work. There might be the potential to make free riding a full-time endeavor, if not an actual lifestyle.

My nickname came about in '95, following a race in Washington State. I was hanging out in my hotel room, smoking some weed, and watching a National Geographic program on wombats. There was a knock on the door. A couple of riders said there was a party and wanted to know if was interested in joining them.

"No thanks. I'm cool right here," I said.

"What are you doing?"

"Just watching this show about wombats."

They looked at each other and laughed.

I didn't care. I was baked as hell, and totally into the furry little dudes.

"Wombats," I could hear them say as they walked away. Then there was laughter. "Fucking Link."

After that I became Larry "the Wombat" Linkogle. SMP jumped all over it, promoting me as the Wombat and even using the name on some of their gear. That's when things got a little strange. I appreciated everything that SMP had done for me; I truly respected the company, especially Brian Manley, for having the guts to get behind a guy who wasn't exactly beloved by the motocross industry. SMP had the foresight to anticipate a coming revolution, and I was part of that revolution. But let's be honest—it wasn't like I was making a ton of money. At first I didn't care, but when I started seeing kids wearing T-shirts and caps emblazoned with the word "Wombat," I felt a pang of resentment. If SMP was gaining popularity (at least in part) because of what the free riders were doing, then it seemed reasonable to think it might be time to talk about changing the structure of our arrangement.

But that didn't happen. Instead, SMP really got its claws into us and began exercising greater control over what we could wear and what type of equipment we could use and what our bikes would look like. I should have seen it coming, of course, and I understand it better now. The more money there is at stake, the less room there is for freedom of expression and disregard for a corporate mentality. Once again, it seemed, someone else was in control of what I wanted to do, and how I was going to do it.

On the surface, it probably seemed like a great idea to the guys at SMP. They had arranged some sort of deal in which a few of their riders would perform an exhibition during a big supercross event in San Diego, California.

Nathan, Tommy, and I would not race; instead, we'd give the fans a glimpse into the world of freestyle motocross—jumping the supercross triples and trying to execute tricks and jumps on the course. The thinking was this: fans seem to love it when riders do a celebratory trick after a race, so why not give them ten minutes of tricks? They'll eat it up, right?

Wrong.

I knew it was risky. A supercross course is short and tight, with more jumps and more turns and obstacles. But the jumps aren't really set up for executing complicated tricks. There just isn't enough room to gather sufficient speed or momentum. We'd all been doing incredible tricks and monster jumps in the desert and hills around Temecula, but this was a whole different scenario. There was the very real possibility of failing miserably, a fact surely not lost on the AMA. To this day, I think race organizers in San Diego agreed to the exhibition not because they thought fans would love it, but because they were confident we'd fall flat on our faces—literally and figuratively. To hedge their bets, they didn't even let us practice, just put us out there during intermission, ice cold, and basically said, "Go ahead, guys, give 'em a show."

It went just about as bad as I had anticipated. Nathan was barely even a dirt bike guy at the time, so he was somewhat overwhelmed by the technical nature of the course; not surprisingly, he couldn't even complete a triple. I got off one decent trick, but spent most of my time aborting various attempts and simply trying to get from one jump to another. Tommy didn't fare much better. All of this was witnessed by more than thirty thousand eerily silent motocross fans who must have wondered what the fuck the big deal was with freestyle. If this was the best we had to offer, they'd stick with racing, thank you very much.

And who could blame them?

I felt almost sick to my stomach afterward. I was furious with myself for having gone against my better judgment. And now this thing I really cared about . . . this thing that had rekindled my passion for riding—free riding—had been twisted into something unrecognizable. That made me feel awful. And not just because we hadn't been permitted to demonstrate what we could really do, and thus failed as athletes and performers, but because this sport that I loved and that was permitting me to be who I really was, now suddenly seemed to be restrictive.

"I won't ever do anything like that again," I said to Nathan afterward. "They made us look like fools."

With the 1996 outdoor nationals approaching, and knowing the exposure that would come with the event, I decided to request a meeting with some of the brass at SMP. I started with Brian Manley, since I knew he was a good dude, and I felt like I could trust him.

"Your company is doing great," I began. "It's a lot bigger than when we started. And my name is on a lot of your clothing and gear. Don't get me wrong. I'm totally grateful for what you guys have done for me . . . but I want a raise."

I had no idea how he would react. Like I said, I wasn't the confrontational type, and it made me uncomfortable to ask for more money. But it wasn't like I was trying to break the bank or anything. I just wanted a small increase, maybe a royalty on clothing bearing the Wombat logo—something that at least acknowledged that I was an important part of their marketing strategy.

"Absolutely," Brian said, so quickly that I was actually startled.

"Really?"

He nodded.

"You deserve it, Link. I'll go to bat for you. Wait here, okay?"

He returned a few minutes later with one of the company's owners. I felt pretty good about the whole thing, especially when Brian pitched the deal, pleading my case in such a way that I thought for sure we'd be out of there with a handshake agreement in a matter of minutes. Apparently, though, I had overestimated my value; or I'd misjudged the owner's capacity for greed.

Regardless, he listened intently, then sort of shrugged his shoulders and said, "Can't do it, guys. Not enough money in the budget."

Brian and I both sat there in stunned silence. I was more hurt than angry. The guy seemed completely dismissive. Here I thought we were all working for the same team, and clearly that wasn't the case. SMP was growing like crazy, bigger names, faster riders, making deep inroads into the motocross audience, pretty much expanding their brand in every way. Obviously I wasn't responsible for all of that, but I'd played a significant part. And now the owner of the company was big timing me.

"Are you serious?" I asked. "No money in the budget?"

He shook his head. "Sorry."

And that was it. The meeting ended, Brian apologized, told me things would work out eventually, and then they went back to work. I went out for a ride, my ass still sore from the kicking.

———

The motocross nationals were being held at Glen Helen Raceway in San Bernardino, California. One day prior to the competition, there was a huge autograph show at Chaparral Motorsports, one of the biggest motorcycle shops in the state, located on I-215 just ten miles from Glen Helen Raceway. The idea, of course, was to hype the event by giving fans who had flocked to the area from all over the country an opportunity to meet their favorite riders. Most of the top athletes in both the 125 cc and 250 cc classes had been invited to appear at the autograph show. I'd been invited, too, despite the fact that I wasn't a top-ten rider or anything; hell, I wasn't even a top-forty rider by this time. But thanks to the growing popularity of SMP, the company now had the clout to insist that its boys be included in publicity events such as this. I wanted no part of it, to be perfectly honest, but SMP made it clear that my presence was required. And so, like a disgruntled employee, I drove on up to Chaparral with Nathan Fletcher, determined to put my own weird stamp on the proceedings.

"Fuck this, man!" I said to Nathan. "We can't go up there looking like a bunch of fucking dorks again, the way we did at San Diego. We need to make a statement."

"What do you have in mind?"

I remembered that my dad had some old war paint in the garage, stuff buried in an old shoe box that he'd brought back from Vietnam. Why he'd never thrown it out, I have no idea. But it was there, just waiting for the right opportunity.

"I'm gonna paint my face for the show."

Nathan started laughing.

"Oh, dude . . . that would be so cool, like the ultimate 'Fuck you!'"

"Totally, right? That's what I'm thinking, too. Fuck you guys!"

So I painted one side of my face completely green, the other side completely black. This was about a year after *Braveheart* had come out, so I was after that sort of warrior look and spirit. Mainly, though, I just wanted to make it clear that I was not like everyone else who would be appearing at the show. Motocross autograph shows are all about glitter and flames; I was going for grunge. The AMA hated it, of course, as did my fellow competitors, but the fans ate it up.

On the way back, Nathan and I were totally stoked, not about motocross, but about coming up with some sort of master plan to wreak havoc on the motocross industry by behaving in a way that would make the establishment squirm. We would create a propaganda machine designed to make free riding look appealing, and traditional motocross boring and stodgy. Anyone with an ounce of cool in their blood would prefer the former. I'm not saying we were geniuses; we were more like Bill and Ted on an angry fucking adventure of mayhem and madness.

"We need a name for our propaganda machine," I said.

"Yeah, Dude," Nathan said. He paused. "I got it! How about the Metal Militia?"

"Oh, man . . . that is fucking awesome. The Metal Militia!"

There was silence.

"What's it mean?" I wondered aloud.

Nathan said nothing. Then he began bobbing his head slowly, like he'd come up with the perfect answer.

"If anybody asks, we'll just say, 'Metal Militia—it's nothing now, but one day it'll be something!'"

"Dude! That is fucking brilliant!"

"Yeah."

In a way, it actually was kind of brilliant. Nathan and I had been talking for a while about sponsorships and endorsements, and how strange it was to see all these kids dressing like us, wearing the same gear we wore when competing. We realized that it didn't matter who produced the gear; we were the only brand that mattered. Eventually we'd figure out how to combine our disdain for the mainstream motocross world with a legitimate business plan. Anger and frustration actually fueled a viable company.

As for the name . . . well, as far as I can recall, it had something to do with the fact that Nathan was a big Metallica fan, and "Metal Militia" was a Metallica song. I guess it just popped into his head that day. I'd like to tell you we chose an alternate spelling to avoid copyright infringement, but that isn't what happened. The truth is, when we scratched out the first logo that very day, neither one of us knew how to spell "militia."

"Just spell it the way it sounds," I suggested.

And so, in true Beavis and Butthead fashion, we ended up with Metal Mulisha, a company that today is a leader in the action sports industry, with annual sales of more than $30 million. At first, though, it was more like a club for me and my friends. We'd wear spiked shoulder pads and camouflage pants. We'd use thick black markers to write "Metal Mulisha" on our shirts and on the sides of our bikes. People would come up to me at freestyle events and ask, "Dude, cool logo. What's it mean? Is it a clothing line?"

"Uhhh . . . I don't know. Maybe."

"What do you mean, maybe? What's the Metal Mulisha?"

I'd smile and nod.

"It's nothing yet, but one day it's gonna be something!"

On the way back from the autograph show at Chaparral, we passed a limousine carrying five or six of the top riders. We were so disgusted. Rolling to an autograph show in a fucking limo? Are you kidding me? For motocross riders? Shit, not one of these guys was recognizable on the street, and here they were acting like NASCAR superstars.

"Dude," Nathan said. "We should pull up beside these assholes, and you should show them your dick."

"Uh, yeah, obviously!"

So Nathan slowed his old white van and allowed the limo to come alongside us, and there, right out in the middle of the freeway, with my face painted green and black, I dropped my trousers and gave them the middle finger. The windows were tinted, but I'm pretty sure I could see them all just shaking their heads.

═══════

I showed up at Glen Helen the next day with a big chip on my shoulder. The autograph show had gone well, despite my attempts at sabotage, and now everyone from SMP was excited about what might happen at the nationals. On an outdoor track I was fast enough to at least perform competitively, so the SMP logo would be visible and my name would be called over the PA system often enough to legitimize the company from both a creative and competitive standpoint.

"This is the day, Larry," SMP's owner said to me that morning. "We're gonna show 'em. We're going to take over this industry!"

Yeah, right . . .

I went to the starting line with his words in my head, coupled with the memory of our recent negotiations. SMP wanted to pay its serious racers three times what they were paying me, even though I was arguably the most popular "brand" in their clothing line. I couldn't get over the notion that they were basically laughing at me; they were cashing in on my popularity, and the budding free-riding movement that I had helped create, and yet they didn't feel my contributions were worth compensating.

We're going to take over the industry?

Fuck you!

I looked down at the starting line, across the row of riders in their glistening uniforms, on their pristine bikes, and I was filled suddenly with a sense of disgust. I'd felt it in the past at various times: a complete and utter disinterest in competing, and something like contempt for the sport itself. I felt confined, constricted. When I was younger and felt this way, I usually just gave up or simply rode badly. More recently it had played out in the form of general craziness on the track: occasional jumps and dangerously aggressive riding. Now, though, I felt something stronger, a need to take all this anger and funnel it into something bigger. I thought of the debacle at San Diego, and I felt a rush of shame. These people had no idea what I could do on a bike. Maybe it was time to show them. Rather than going out and finishing maybe third in my qualifier and fiftieth in the finals, I would try to make a point. I would turn the outdoor nationals into a freestyle demonstration.

I would go out not with a whimper, but with a bang. With one massive, final "Fuck off!"

The gate dropped. While everyone else hit the throttle and jockeyed for position, racing to the first turn, I just cruised casually to the back of the pack, doing little wheelies, letting the field pull away.

Brap-brap-brap-brap.

Having practiced on the course, I knew the layout featured at least a few jumps that could be utilized for tricks, so I just let everyone else go off and race, figuring I'd ride just fast enough to avoid getting lapped, but not so fast as to become part of the pack. In other words, I'd have the track to myself. So I rolled into the first jump and—boom!—Double Can Can. Both legs hanging off the side of the bike. In the years since, this little trick has become almost like a warm-up maneuver for freestylers. It's that common, that basic. But in 1996, it was practically brand new. And in this context—in front of some fifty thousand people who had come to witness a motocross race featuring the fastest riders in the world—it was shocking, if not downright revolutionary. There was no YouTube; hell, there was barely an Internet. Cell phones were not equipped with cameras. The unusual did not become mundane overnight, the way it does now. A few hardcore fans had probably seen some of the *Crusty Demon* videos, but for the most part, this was a crowd of traditionalists. They probably thought I was crazy.

I can still remember the sound—complete silence as I flew through the air. And then an incredible roar as my bike hit the ground. I'd been riding for almost decade, and I'd never felt or heard anything like that. I was so amped.

Whoa, much better, dude!

Honest to God, I don't think I would have felt that good if I'd won the nationals.

So I kept right on going. Second jump—let go with both hands . . . and both legs! The place began to freak out. Next jump, another trick. Followed by another. By the end of the second lap, people were pushed up against the edge of the track, cheering me on as if I were one of the leaders of the race. I didn't have a strategy for any of this. It was spontaneous, and I even figured I'd be off the track within a minute or two of hitting my first trick. Instead, I completed the entire race, nailing jump after jump with the crowd going nuts the whole time. And I remember feeling a swell of pride as I cruised into the pits after the race ended; a sense of validation. I had stolen the show, and that in itself was an accomplishment.

"Dude, that was so fucking sick," Nathan Fletcher said. "Listen to these people! They're stoked!"

Not everyone appreciated it. The other riders were pissed, the race organizers were pissed, and even the owner of SMP was pissed.

"You didn't even try out there," he said, shaking his head in disgust.

I didn't care. They wanted me to be their poster boy? Fine, I'd give them more than they bargained for.

"Didn't you hear everyone screaming?" I said. "They loved it!"

He just walked away. Apparently I had crossed a line. What SMP wanted was a bad boy image, without actually having to deal with a bad boy. They wanted me to pretend to be some sort of rebel, but on race day I was supposed to conform and be like everyone else. I couldn't do it.

After that qualifier I spent the rest of the day getting hugely fucked up. I wasn't much of a drinker, but that day I got completely shit-faced. People kept coming up to me, congratulating me, telling me they'd never seen anything like it, wanting to know when and where I'd be riding again. I turned my SMP shirt inside out and used a Sharpie to write "Metal Mulisha" on the chest. I'm pretty sure I wrote some other real sinister, nasty shit, as well. At some point one of the fans asked me for my shirt, so I gave it to him. I had no tattoos at the time, so I inked myself with the Sharpie, writing "Fuck Off!" on my skin. I'd walk into the pit crews of other racers and start punking them.

"Dude, how's the race going? You got twenty-third place? Cool. Good for you. How's that training going? Keep working hard, maybe you can finish in the top twenty."

I was a total asshole. And I did not care. I don't say that with pride. I'm just trying to relate my mindset at the time. I'm trying to be honest. I had hijacked the outdoor nationals, and fifty thousand people had voiced their approval. I realized then that there was an audience for free riding . . . or freestyle . . . or whatever you wanted to call it. It was a defining moment in my life. The thing I loved—the thing I was good at—had value.

It would be arrogant and self-aggrandizing to suggest that this was the day freestyle motocross was born. For years guys had been executing tricks and riding purely for the joy of it, usually far from the crowds or the video cameras. I hopped on the wave, adapted a few new tricks, and embraced it as a lifestyle. No single person can take credit for "creating" freestyle—the movement was organic and widespread. But if you want to pick one day, one moment, when the free-riding movement elbowed its way into the spotlight and became something more than a sideshow . . . well, this one is as good as any.

I made a decision that day: I was done with racing. I was done with motocross and the AMA and all of its stick-up-the-ass rules and regulations. From now on, I was a freestyler, a free rider.

Full time.

CHAPTER 5

It wasn't like I had some grand and glorious plan for building a freestyle motocross empire. I was just happy to be riding without constraints or expectations (other than those I placed upon myself). I bulldozed a big section of my supercross track, put in some gigantic jumps, and started having fun again, just riding every day in my own backyard, not worrying about whether I'd win the next race or whether I was dressed properly or anything like that. I just wanted to ride with my buddies, catch big air, and develop new tricks. It was very much a skateboarder's approach to the game. But never in that process—never in a million years—did I say to myself, *"Hey, I'm going to take this and make it the next big action sport!"* I was just trying to recapture some of the enjoyment that had been sucked out of riding. Simple as that.

The thing is, word quickly spread about what we were doing, and that fueled a lot of interest. A motocross racer and future freestyler named Shane Trittler promoted the first freestyle event in 1996 in Castaic, California, and I finished first. I didn't really give a shit about winning; I was just happy to be part of something that seemed to be taking on a life of its own, and that people really enjoyed.

You know what else was satisfying? My parents came to accept what I was doing. Mom had always been pretty supportive and understanding, and now my father seemed to have a different outlook as well. Part of this transformation had nothing to do with me; by this time, my father had become a very different man, thanks to therapy and counseling and whatever other services he was receiving from the VA. He was a far more patient and tolerant person than the one I'd known while growing up. He'd thrown himself totally into the vineyard by this point, and with that immersion came a distancing from my motocross career. He no longer seemed to care one way or the other what I was doing with my life, athletically speaking.

I know that my parents were disappointed with my antics in the early days of the freestyle movement. They didn't like the videos, the partying, the vulgar slogans splashed across my bike. But when they saw what happened at the outdoor nationals at Glen Helen, and the response my performance provoked, they began to come around. Maybe their son wasn't a loser after all. Maybe he wasn't a punk. Maybe he was onto something. I also think my dad came to understand that I wasn't happy when I was racing motocross; I was happy free riding and doing tricks. I liked entertaining crowds. Eventually I think he just stopped trying to make me something I wasn't and accepted me for who I was.

The fact that I ended up being successful obviously helped ease the sting of disappointment. I understand now how hard it must have been for him. I had grown up in the motocross community, which meant my father was pretty well known within the industry. Many of his friends were the parents of my fellow competitors. I can only imagine how he felt when I would show up dressed like Elvis and then deliberately sabotage a race. Rather than become a laughing-stock, he pulled away from the sport completely and left me to my own devices. When it turned out that freestyle wasn't merely a gimmick, but an enormously popular sport, he must have been shocked.

But he also was proud.

My father ended up being a big supporter of my freestyle career. Once I made a decision to stop racing, he never told me I was wrong, never pressured me to return to the circuit. He became a fan, and that meant the world to me. He even helped me transform the motocross course on our property into the first-of-its-kind freestyle course in the world. Working closely with me, Brian Manley, and my boyhood hero, Micky Dymond, we created a freestyle mecca for riders from all over the country.

Micky was the coolest guy in motocross racing when I was growing up, a racer who really broke the mold in the 1980s. In a sport that was relatively straight-laced, Micky was something of a renegade. He had long hair, tattoos, hung out and partied with the guys from Mötley Crüe, and always had hot chicks trailing after him. Micky could party and do drugs and it didn't seem to affect his riding. He'd show up at the track with his buddy Nikki Sixx, looking all strung out, and still kick everyone's ass at nationals. And occasionally he'd celebrate with a big jump afterward, just to entertain the crowd. So Micky had the respect of the traditional motocross industry because he was so incredibly talented and successful, and he was admired by the freestylers because he was so gnarly.

Micky saw what we were doing and wanted to be a part of it. And I couldn't have been happier to work with him. We hit it off right away, became close friends, and I still consider him one of my best friends.

Micky basically did the whole design for my course. It was brilliant. He designed universal jumps that could be positioned in different ways, allowing for two riders to jump at the same time, crossing in mid-air. He built a model of the entire course out of cardboard and clay (I still have the original), and then we began pushing dirt all over the place.

Before long, photographers and journalists wanted to come out and shoot at my house and do stories about the sport's surging popularity. But I restricted access to the folks who hadn't treated me like some sort of pariah. I found it interesting that the same magazines that had published editorials calling me a "degenerate" and a "disgrace to the sport" suddenly were asking permission to visit my course. And the balls on these guys! Not only would they request access to my home, but they'd ask if they could bring one of the riders from their stable to take part in the photo shoot.

"Hey, Link . . . mind if we come out with Jeremy McGrath tomorrow?"

"Uhhh . . . yeah, actually I *do* mind."

Mainly the course was reserved for me and my friends, which served only to stoke the fire. Before long, there were sponsors interested in partnering with some of the freestylers. The guys at Fleshwound Films kept cranking out titles in the *Crusty Demons* series, each more popular than the one that preceded it. A *Crusty Demons* tour soon followed, and before I knew it, I had the greatest job ever: traveling around the world, filming videos, and taking part in exhibition shows where we all tried to outdo each other with bigger and better tricks. Then everything exploded, much as it had in BMX, skateboarding, and snowboarding. Top professional racers—big-name guys—started going out and doing freestyle. And they weren't doing it for the money—not in the beginning, anyway. They were doing it because it was fun; it was different. At the end of the day, whether you're a racer or a freestyler, if you like riding a motorcycle, you like jumping. That's why we all got into it when we were kids. And if you're talented, the jumps get bigger and more creative. It's a common ground. Everyone can relate to it.

Within a few short years, freestyle motocross had become one of the biggest action sports, with showcases and competitions and prize money and sponsorships. People loved it! And why not? It featured all the acrobatic and creative elements of skateboarding, BMX, and snowboarding—but with significantly more danger. If you want to progress in freestyle, you can't look at the consequences, and you can't be scared of getting hurt; you can't focus on what might happen five minutes from now. You have to live in the moment. We all know that. Nevertheless, the reality for every freestyle motocross rider is that you are going to get badly fucked up. There's no way around it. There's not a serious motocross guy out there who hasn't suffered multiple broken bones and torn ligaments. It comes with the territory, more so than in any other sport.

I'm not minimizing the risks of BMX, snowboarding, or skateboarding. The difference is they're not covering eighty-five-foot gaps, while soaring thirty-five feet in the air. If you mess up in freestyle motocross, you can't just roll out of it or ride on your knees or toss your board into some powder. You have one chance to hit the jump properly, and if you don't do it right, not only are you going to get slammed from three or four stories in the air onto rock-hard dirt, you've got a three-hundred-pound bike chasing you all the way down.

So the lifespan of a freestyle rider is freakishly short. Maybe five to seven years, tops. At best. And much of that time will be spent recuperating from injuries, ignoring the injuries, or getting loaded on painkillers to help you deal with the injuries. I went through two years of performing and competing, all the time suffering from a smashed meniscus and a torn ACL in my knee and a separated shoulder. Never took time off during that period. It's not like other professional sports where you have disability insurance and sick time. There's no union running action sports. If you're not riding, you're not getting paid.

Money was not a driving force in my life when I started riding bikes, and it wasn't a prime motivational factor when I started freestyling. Still, you have to pay the bills, right? And you want to feel like you're being fairly compensated for your effort and ability. Like so many things about my riding career, the Metal Mulisha was born out of a desire for autonomy and independence. And eventually it really did become *something*, just as Nathan Fletcher and I had hoped when we came up with the idea in '96. What began as a collection of riders bound by a love of freestyle and a loosely defined mission to rebel against the motocross mainstream, evolved into a legitimate business.

When Nathan lost interest in the late 1990s and took off to go surfing in Tahiti for a while, Brian Deegan became my new road dog and riding partner. He was a terrific freestyler and a smart guy, and we shared an affinity for partying that fueled our friendship for a number of years (and ultimately led to a spectacularly acrimonious breakup and litigation that continues to this day; much more on that later). Together we formed an LLC, started producing some T-shirts with the Mulisha logo, and before long our little company mushroomed into something I never could have imagined.

The Metal Mulisha progressed quickly right alongside the sport of freestyle motocross. Within just a few short years, the popularity of freestyle had eclipsed that of traditional motocross, and with those changes came responsibilities that frankly I hadn't anticipated. I was something of a pioneer in the sport, among the first group of stars. And yet, almost before I had a chance to react, there were hot-shot kids from all over the world doing tricks I'd never envisioned.

I remember doing a photo shoot for a magazine out of France in 1998. They came to my house and brought with them some prodigy, a young Spaniard who could do remarkable tricks on his motorcycle. The idea was for the two of us to ride together, nudging each other along all day, pushing each other to greater heights. It was a perfect winter morning, sunny and clear, with snow-capped peaks off in the distance—a magazine photographer's wet dream of a setting. It had rained the previous day, too, which made the earth nice and loose, so we could groom the course neatly. By the time we started riding, conditions were just about ideal. We were introduced, shook hands, nodded out of mutual respect, but really couldn't communicate at all because of the language barrier. A funny thing happened. As soon as we started warming up, I felt my competitive juices beginning to flow. How fucking weird is that? I'd stopped racing at least partly because my competitive fire had been extinguished. And now here I was, in a simple photo shoot, trying to protect my turf and show this hotshot kid from Spain that he had a few things to learn.

Dude, this is how we roll in California.

It was my backyard, so naturally I was dialed in right from the start. I knew every inch of the course, every bump and rut. Seeing as he showed up with pristine gear, and was accompanied by an entourage that included his mother, I was also pretty sure that I had bigger balls than this kid. I hit one jump after another, all clean, kept stretching it out farther, until I finally felt loose enough to break out the Double Can Can, my go-to trick.

Bam! Nailed that shit!

Then, just for good measure, I ran the biggest jump on the course a couple times.

Your turn, kid. Step up!

Man, I was cocky. I figured I had completely stolen the photo shoot. I thought he might just pack it in right there and go home. Instead, he more than rose to the challenge, perfectly hitting the biggest jump on the course, same one I'd hit a few minutes earlier. Then he did it again, this time throwing in a trick for good measure.

Uh-oh . . . Game on.

He wasn't finished either. The kid went after the big jump a third time, hit the takeoff with pinpoint precision and soared into the air. I watched in awe as the kid released his grip on the handlebars, placed his palms on the seat of the bike, and then extended his feet out behind him.

Oh, shit. Superman . . .

A trick first popularized by Jeremy McGrath, the Superman gave the impression of a rider in full flight, not so much riding his bike as trailing it through the sky. McGrath had done the Superman at the end of races and in exhibitions, and it always killed. But he'd never done a Superman like this. No one had ever done it like this. The goal when executing a Superman was to simply go horizontal, at 180 degrees, while barely touching the bike. But this kid had gone way beyond horizontal. Rather than just kicking his feet out behind him, he'd lifted his legs high in the air, his boots hanging back over his body, two feet above his torso, like a scorpion getting ready to strike. He held the position for what seemed like an eternity. As the bike sailed across the open air, he seemed almost to be doing a handstand on the seat. It was freakishly acrobatic and impressive, and more than a little dangerous.

And then it was done. The kid pulled his legs back onto the bike, grabbed the handlebars, and hit the ground perfectly. Barely even bounced. Everyone started applauding and cheering. Even my buddies. Hell, I felt like clapping myself. But all I could do was sit there on my bike, staring at this kid who had basically just shut me down.

Fuck! What am I gonna do now?

That's the way it went for most of the day, a Spanish teenager kicking my ass in my own backyard. And it wasn't just that he was talented and creative. This kid had clearly been practicing. He'd been training. To my way of thinking, that was like a violation of the freestyle code. Hell, I'd gotten out of racing because I hated practice! I just wanted to ride and have fun. But this kid had a different view on things. He took the sport seriously and approached it with precisely the same degree of professionalism and intensity you'd expect from any elite athlete. And he was doing stuff I'd never seen—stuff *nobody* had ever seen.

In the end, I saved a measure of dignity by doing a huge transfer jump, almost two hundred feet, and he wouldn't even try that. But I realized something had changed, that I could no longer get by on talent alone. The sport I'd helped create was threatening to pass me by. So after the Spaniard and the photo crew left, I fired up my bike and kept riding, trying to replicate some of the tricks this kid had been doing, and even experimenting with some gnarly new tricks of my own, including one that involved sticking my feet through the handlebars, then letting go of the bars and whipping my feet back around behind me. Almost like something you'd see a gymnast do on a pommel horse. Except I was trying to do it at forty miles per hour, on a motorcycle, while flying through the air. The trick would eventually be dubbed a Saran Wrap and become a standard weapon in the freestyler's arsenal. At this point, though, it was experimental, and I botched the experiment.

I remember going up, sticking my foot through the bars, and then my hand getting pinned beneath my legs, so that I couldn't complete the move; effectively hog-tied to the bike, I felt a sensation of utter helplessness as the ground rushed up before me. I had no control whatsoever, no way to stop the impending disaster.

Oh, this is going to be bad . . .

The concussive force of the crash knocked me out for a few brief seconds, or what felt like a few seconds, anyway. When I came to, the bike was on top of me, with the handlebars wedged against my stomach. I pushed the bike away and felt a sharp tug in my abdomen. And then I felt something wet and warm running down my crotch and legs. I reached down with my hand; through my glove I could feel something weird beneath my jersey, a lump of some sort near my naval. Pain radiated across my torso, but I was so disoriented and weak that I couldn't figure out exactly what was happening. I remember hearing one of my riding buddies standing over me asking if I was okay, and then I could hear him yelling for help. And then my father was at my side, holding my hand.

"Dad? I just want to sleep, okay? Get me in the house."

My father rushed me to the hospital in his Corvette. The last thing I clearly remember is him driving really fast, and the sight of blood everywhere. I faded in and out of consciousness as we pulled up to the hospital. There were doctors and nurses rushing all about as they pulled me into the ER and began cutting off my clothes. I remember someone freaking out about my blood pressure and then everything turned real bright.

And then the lights went out.

━━━━━━

I woke up in the intensive care unit of Inland Valley Hospital surrounded by a collection of folks in really bad shape, virtually all of them unconscious, and some on life support. For the first twenty-four hours, no visitors were allowed. It would be a while before I got the full details of the accident and its aftermath. I learned that I'd been impaled on the handlebars, which had ripped right through my clothing and my skin and deep into my abdominal muscles and intestines before popping back out. Several hours of surgery had been required to put everything back together, and to scoop out my spleen, which apparently had exploded upon impact. I didn't know any of this when I first woke up in the ICU; I knew only that I was in a world of hurt, and that I couldn't move an inch. The slightest shift in my body weight produced ripples of pain throughout my torso. A nurse gave a perfunctory demonstration on how to use the morphine pump by my side, and it quickly became my best friend. I maxed it out every fifteen minutes, trying to squelch the pain and put myself to sleep.

"Can I get some water?" I said to the nurse in a voice barely above a whisper. There was a tube down my throat—speaking made me feel like I was going to gag. And I was thirsty—the worst cotton mouth I'd ever experienced.

"Sorry," she said coolly. "No water. Doctor's orders."

I remember pleading. She refused again, and I remember wondering why she was being such a bitch to a guy who had just come out of surgery after practically killing himself in a motorcycle accident.

"Please . . ." I rasped.

She left the room and returned a few minutes later with a Styrofoam cup filled with ice cubes and a small amount of water, placed it on the table by my bed, so all I could do was watch the ice melt and the condensation pool around the base of the cup. It looked so refreshing, so tantalizing. I tried to slide forward in bed a few inches, thinking I could grab the cup with my fingertips.

Ahhhhhhh!

My body shivered with pain.

The nurse came back again, shook her head in admonishment, and held out three cotton swabs—each roughly the size of a toothpick with a tiny square sponge at the tip. One by one, she inserted these little cheese-wedge cotton swabs into the ice water, then tapped them against the rim of the cup to drain any excess moisture. Then she handed them to me.

"Suck on these," she said.

And so I did, teasing every little drop of liquid out of each.

The following morning, my parents were allowed to visit for the first time, and I told them how badly I'd been treated, how the nurse had not only taunted me with the cup of water but had seemed to take perverse pleasure in witnessing my pain.

"Larry, was this a big lady with short hair?"

"Yeah, why?"

"We spoke with her last night," my mother explained. "Apparently you said some really nasty things to her when you came out of surgery."

"I did? Like what?"

My mother shook her head. "I'd rather not say."

Eventually my father told me that I had unleashed a torrent or profanity and vulgarity on this poor woman (including remarks about her sexual preference), and she had been more than a little offended. I've since discovered that this is an unfortunate but not uncommon side effect of anesthesia: some people behave like complete assholes when they first begin to shake the effects of anesthesia. I am one of those people. I've had a number of surgical procedures since that time, and I've always made it a point to explain to everyone at the hospital that they should be prepared for a personality transformation.

"Look, I have this problem. When I wake up from the anesthesia, I'm probably going to say some mean and bad things, and cuss you out, but I don't mean it; I really don't. And I'm sorry. Please don't hold it against me."

I spent a week in the ICU and another two or three weeks after that in the hospital. The whole time I was there I was doped up on morphine. As a bonus, they sent me home with a ton of painkillers, a veritable jug of Vicodin, which

I popped every four to six hours round the clock as prescribed. I had my own house by this time, abutting the motocross course on my father's property, but since I couldn't really take care of myself, I moved back into the guest house at my parents' place while recovering from the injury. At first, I could barely get around at all. I used a walker and moved like a ninety-year-old man, shuffling along, hunched over the frame, my breathing labored, my muscles so atrophied that they could barely support my weight. Even today, I walk sort of crooked, the residual effect of spending months with my body bent at a forty-five-degree angle.

The instructions were simple: relax, heal, take everything slow. Forget about getting back on the bike—that was many months down the road. I didn't believe them, of course. I figured I'd been through accidents and injuries in the past and always managed to recover pretty quickly; this would be no different. Within a few weeks after getting home, I was hanging out with my new girlfriend, Crystal, rolling with my buddies. I ignored the doctors' advice, and before long I began to experience complications. There was, for example, a growing knot on my stomach, just an inch or two from my surgical zipper. Of course, it wasn't really *on* my stomach; it was *in* my stomach. At first, it was a little scary looking but painless. In time, it started to throb. And grow. What started out as a small marble-sized lump swelled to the size of a golf ball . . . and then to the size of a baseball.

I didn't tell anyone about it for a while. I'm weird like that. I don't always reveal when I'm hurt or have something going on. I keep it to myself. Not just to prevent others from worrying about me, but also because I tend to deny the obvious—until there's no other option but to deal with it. I reached that point when the lump turned purple and hot—like a giant boil—and began oozing a thick pink liquid.

"Mom," I said one day. "Can you take a look at this?"

Predictably, she freaked out and insisted on taking me straight to the emergency room. The doc took one look at the lump on my stomach and said, "This isn't good. You have an infection in there."

Here's the way I understand it: wounds need to heal from the inside out, and since I had basically been stabbed, and the wound had been so deep, the process was more complicated than usual. The infection had started deep in my body, and now was bubbling to the surface, as the wound tried to cleanse itself by pushing out all the puss and blood and bacterial matter. The lump was essentially a volcano of toxic sludge preparing to erupt.

"We'll have to clean it out," the doc explained. "But you'll be fine afterward."

I figured, *Okay, cool, bring me back to the surgical suite, put me under, give me some more drugs, and take care of business.* Instead, the doctor put on one of those big welding masks that surgeons use when they expect a procedure to be particularly messy. Then he called for a nurse and picked up a scalpel.

Uh-oh. That got my attention.

"What? You mean, like . . . right now?!"

"Yes," he said. "This thing needs to be cleaned immediately. You're at serious risk for gangrene." He paused. "You could die, son."

"Yeah, I get that," I stammered. "But do I have to be awake?"

"You'll be fine," he said. "You won't feel a thing."

The fuck I won't!

"Just a little pressure, maybe some tugging and pulling."

There are always risks associated with anesthesia, and in my case, he explained very briefly, the risks outweighed the benefits. The nerves around the wound were damaged anyway, and so much pressure had built up inside the wound that a simple slice would do the trick. So there was no epidural, no gas, no sedatives of any kind. Not even a shot of Novocain.

"Be very still," he said. "It'll be over quickly."

Gaaaaaaaa!

As promised, there was no pain, but I sure as hell could feel him in there, digging around, pushing and pulling, sucking shit out. I could feel something dripping down my belly, and I could smell the awful stench of infection. My mom stood by my side the whole time; only later did she admit that she had nearly passed out.

Afterward, as they cleaned me up, I looked down to get a glimpse of the doc's handiwork. There was a three-inch gash in my skin, and beneath that, a huge, open pocket where the infectious lump had been lodged. Now, though, the wound was clean, and I could see clearly the various layers of my body: pink flesh, white muscle, gray intestines, all neatly stacked on top of each other. To my amazement, he did not stitch the wound closed, but instead packed it with gauze and sent me on my way.

"That needs to be changed every six hours," the doc explained.

I nodded. "So I come back here tonight?"

"No, you can do it yourself."

What?! I can't do this myself! That's what hospitals are for!

That's what I thought, anyway. What I said was, "Okay." I just wanted to go home and sleep.

For the first week or so, I couldn't bring myself to change the dressing. The whole idea of sticking my hand inside my own stomach totally freaked me out. So I relied on others to help, and to show me how it was done. That day I drove over to my friend Colin Yates' house. Colin's mother was a nurse, so I figured she'd know what to do. She had me lay down on the kitchen counter, while Colin watched, and proceeded to change the dressing like a pro.

"Oh, man, I gotta record this," Colin said, holding a video camera over my stomach. "This is sick!"

Mrs. Yates expertly began tugging at the dressing. I had no idea what was involved, assumed there was the equivalent of a couple cotton balls stuffed into the wound.

"Just relax, Larry," she said. "Try not to move."

She took the end of the gauze between her fingertips and slowly reeled it in, wrapping the excess around her hand as it came out. Two inches . . . four inches . . . six . . . a foot! It reminded me of that magic trick where the magician pulls a seemingly endless ribbon of tissue out of his mouth. A gimmick simultaneously mesmerizing and repulsive. When all the gauze had been removed, Mrs. Yates cleaned the wound, repacked it with fresh gauze, and put a fresh bandage on the outside.

"There you go, hon," she said. "Good as new."

Well, not quite.

For the next six months I walked around with a hole in my stomach, and during that entire time I took pain medication pretty much round the clock. I wasn't abusing the meds or anything. I mean, I took them strictly to cope with the pain, not to get some sort of high. But the truth is, my body had developed a fairly serious relationship with opiates. Eventually the wound healed, closing to roughly the size of a silver dollar. There wasn't much pain anymore and I could get around pretty well on my own. I wasn't ready to do any freestyle jumps or anything like that, but I felt pretty good. Oddly enough, though, I began to think about the effects of all that medication; I figured that soon enough it would be time to start the weaning process. Before that happened, though, I wondered what it would it would be like to take painkillers on a recreational basis.

There's no way to rationalize or even explain the thought process behind this decision. It grew out of boredom and recklessness, I suppose, and maybe some deep-seeded desire to inflict damage upon myself. I don't remember worrying about or even weighing the consequences, that's for sure.

It's strange—so much of that year is a blur to me; a haze of surgery and medication and recovery. Endless hours on my back, watching television, the minutes passing like hours. But I remember that day vividly. I remember it like it happened yesterday. I was at Crystal's house, sitting on the couch, a bottle of Vicodin by my side. I'd accrued so much of this shit, more than I needed, more than I could ever hope to use (or so I thought), and now the end of the road was near. Time to toss it out, right? Time to quit.

I removed the cap, flipped the bottle over, and shook it until one of the pills spilled onto my palm. Then a second. I looked at them. Two was the usual dosage; I'd never exceeded that amount.

Hmm . . . when I take two of these little guys, my pain goes away. Wonder what would happen if I took four?

Another little shake; two more pills slid out of the bottle. I washed the whole batch down with some water and sank into the couch, waiting for the drug to kick in. It didn't take long, maybe ten or fifteen minutes. It came on slowly, comfortably, enveloping me like a blanket, or a warm embrace. It was like nothing I'd ever experienced before. I mean, I'd been drunk, stoned, fucked up on ecstasy, weed, and acid. But this was different. This was magnificent! The arms of the sofa seemed to rise up around me, pulling me close, telling me everything would be all right. It felt reassuring, protective, like a hug from my mother or father. And I realized then, this is what I've been missing. This is what I want.

This is what I need.

CHAPTER 6

People always want to know about the tattoos. I don't blame them. You can't have as much ink as I do and not expect to be asked about it once in a while.

The thing is, I never expected it to turn out this way. Like so many other things, body art can be addictive. You start out with a little tattoo in some hidden place, where no one can even see it, and then you wake up twenty years later with a multicolored roadmap of your life splattered across every inch of your body. Tattoos large and small, gnarly and neat, reflecting people you've loved or people you've despised (maybe people you've loved and then despised), places you've been and things you've done; snapshot reminders of acts despicable and heroic or maybe just plain stupid.

Funny thing, though: they always seem like a good idea at the time.

Despite his background, or maybe because of it, my father was a real stickler when it came to tattoos. He'd served in Vietnam, hung out with a lot of hard-ass, nasty-looking dudes, many of whom considered tattoos to be a birthright, and yet his body was completely devoid of ink. Tattoos have always been common in the military, and I suspect they reminded my father of one of the worst periods of his life. In his eyes, tattoos were the province of criminals and thugs and losers of one type or another. A lot of his fellow soldiers had tattoos; a lot of them had drug problems. I suppose my father lumped these things together.

Regardless, he made his feelings on the matter abundantly clear.

"If you ever get a tattoo, I'm going to cut that thing off with a razor blade," he said on more than one occasion.

I'd usually just laugh.

"Come on, Dad. What's the big deal?"

"You think I'm kidding? Try me."

For the longest time I did not even think about challenging my father on this issue. I knew better. A fair number of guys on the motocross circuit had tattoos and eventually I knew I'd be one of them. But it wasn't until I was about seventeen years old, after I'd begun to grow weary of the professional racing scene and pull away from my father, that I finally got my first tattoo. But I did it in a way that exhibited both courage and cowardice. Courage in that I was inked in a manner and place that would make most people squirm; cowardice in that I chose this particular spot to prevent my parents from knowing about it.

Here's the way it went down . . .

I was hanging out with my friend Mike Metzger when the conversation turned to ink. Mike was something of an artist even then, liked to paint and talked frequently about becoming a tattoo artist. He was a hell of a rider, too, an early member of the Metal Mulisha team, and eventually one of the top athletes in freestyle motocross. Pioneered a bunch of great tricks, even once did a backflip over the fountains at Caesars Palace in Las Vegas. Almost killed himself a couple times, too. You see Mike now and he's got tattoos everywhere, just like me; he even opened his own tattoo parlor in Lake Elsinore. The guy is an expert when it comes to ink.

Back in those days, though, we were both virgins, our skin as clear as could be. Mike, though, had somehow gotten his hands on a tattoo kit, and he was itching to put it to use.

"Dude, let me give you a tat," he said. "I'm dying to try this thing."

"No way, man. My father will kill me."

Metzger knew exactly how I felt. His parents had also forbidden him from getting a tattoo.

"But I really want one," he said. "And I want to give you one, too."

And then it came to me: a way to break our tattoo cherries without anyone knowing about it. Unless, of course, we decided to show them.

"Dude, I've got it!" I said. "We can tattoo the insides of our mouths."

Metzger scrunched up his face, as if both disgusted and perplexed.

"What do you mean?"

I grabbed my bottom lip, pulled it away from my gums, and folded it over.

"Right here," I said. "Our parents will never see it."

Mike smiled, nodded. "Yeah, dude . . . totally."

He paused. "What do you want in there?"

I don't know what was going through my head at the time, or why I would have chosen this as my very first tattoo. I suppose a psychologist would have a field day analyzing that one. Anyway, here's what came out of my mouth.

"Why don't you just put 'hate' in there."

So that's exactly what he did. In tiny letters, on the inside of my bottom lip, in dark blue ink, is the word "hate." Metz had a nice touch with the pen, barely even hurt at all. A lot of vibrating, a little stinging, but not nearly as bad as I expected. It's certainly not artistic, and it's not something you can easily explain. But then, most people aren't even aware that I have a tattoo on the inside of my mouth (I'm pretty sure my parents still don't even know, although obviously they will now). I mean, who does that? It's just as well, since I'd rather not have to explain its origin or the motivation behind it. I honestly don't think about it much anymore—too much crazy shit has happened in my life for this to rise high on the list of memorable events.

Sometimes, though, I do find myself tripping on it just a bit—like, what would make me do that? Why would I want the word "hate" inside my mouth? And the only conclusion that can be reached is that even then there must have been a lot of anger inside me. Or stupidity. There's really no other explanation.

I can tell you this: today I barely recognize that kid. But he's left his imprint all over my life and my body. For better or worse. Some people can bury the past . . . hide it. I can't. And I don't even know that I'd want to. It is what it is.

That was it for a while—didn't get another tattoo until a couple years later, but it was a signature job, that's for sure.

At the time I had a really cool helmet, one of my all-time favorites. A friend of mine had done an incredible paint job on this thing, covered it with a picture of a human skull. I loved that helmet and considered it to be something of a lucky charm, as so many good things had happened in my career since I started wearing it. Occasionally I thought about how awesome it would be to have a tattoo on my head that looked like that skull. You know, so that when I removed the helmet, you'd see the same image on my skin. That would freak people out, and since I was into shock value, it appealed to me.

But I didn't act on it. Not right away. Tattoos were totally mainstream among the freestylers and skaters and BMXers, to the point where it didn't even seem that radical to paint your body. I never felt like a joiner anyway, and it seemed on some level that if I started getting a bunch of tattoos, I'd just be following the crowd again. But there was peer pressure, no doubt about it.

A bunch of us started hanging out regularly at a shop in Temecula called Soul Expressions Tattoo. They had opened just a few years earlier, in 1993, and by then had become a favorite tattoo parlor among the motocross crowd. Seth Enslow started going there all the time, got a lot of work done, all of it really first-rate. Ronnie Faisst, another guy who joined the Metal Mulisha stable, has had virtually his entire body inked up at Soul Expressions. I'd be hanging out there, watching all of my friends and riding partners getting painted, and I'd start to get curious. It was an art form, no question about that. And it did make you look like a bit of a badass. Tattoos and motorcycles have always gone together, probably always will go together. But I was a holdout for the longest time.

"Come on, man," the guys at Soul Expressions would say, waving an ink gun in the air. "Let's get you started."

"No fucking way, dude. I ain't ever getting no tattoo. Don't need it."

Of course, this wasn't quite true, as I already had that sloppy little tat on my lower lip. But that one didn't really even count. These guys were into serious ink—the body as a canvas. Or maybe a bulletin board. I didn't feel as though I needed another mode of expression, and to be perfectly candid, I still worried about how my parents would react to my getting a tattoo. It shouldn't have been a big deal, since I was nearly twenty years old at the time. But it was. On some level, I still needed my father's approval.

"Can't do it, guys," I'd say. "My dad will kill me."

Eventually, though, I warmed to the idea. You spend enough time in a tattoo shop, or hanging out with guys who are covered with tattoos, and eventually you're going down that road. And once I decided to take the plunge, I figured I might as well go big. I'd sit around looking at catalogues, or examining the portfolios of the guys at Soul Expression, or just talking with other guys who had ink all over their bodies. After a while the choice seemed obvious.

You know what, man? I'm just going to go for a big ol' head tat.

Let me try to explain the thinking behind this one. It was like I wanted to tear off the mask, to show people what was underneath my face. The real Larry Linkogle would be reflected in a tattoo applied to the back of my skull. Not so much an alter ego (because I was already spending a lot of my time telling everyone to fuck off), but an extreme, evil-ass version of the person I presented to the outside world. I imagined saying something like this to people: "You want to know what I'm really like? Well, here, take a look at this." Then I'd rip off my hat and turn around quickly, and show them the back of my head.

I chose a skull similar to the one that had been painted on my helmet, with ram horns flaring and curling up out of the dome, and a wide, malicious grin. And eyes, too. No lifeless skeleton for me. This would be a living skull, a monster, with the ability to see anyone who might try to sneak up on me from behind. How cool was that?

It wasn't like I invented the idea of a skull tattoo—they've been around forever, or as long as bald guys have been getting ink. A big role model to me at the time, and a very close friend, was Christian Fletcher, Nathan's older brother. Christian was an amazing and innovative surfer, one of the best in history, and a damn good freerider as well. And, like me, he wore his antagonism on his sleeve, freaking out on judges at competitions, breaking other people's surfboards, and generally acting like he just did not give a fuck. Man, that appealed to me. I also liked the fact that beneath Christian's hair, which he sometimes shaved off, was one of the sickest tattoos I'd ever seen: a skull that looked like a cross between a demon and a zombie. You had to have some serious attitude to wear a tattoo like that.

I don't mean to imply that I copied Christian, but he was definitely an inspiration. A head tattoo also seemed logical because I was running a buzz cut at the time anyway, having recently shaved my head after a growing tired of the Bozo the Clown look (nothing on top, curly hair on the sides). So one morning in the middle of the summer, I took a razor and shaved my head right down to the skin. Smooth as a baby's butt. Then I rolled on down to Soul Expression, with helmet in hand, and walked through the door.

"All right," I proclaimed. "I'm ready. Let's get it done."

Kind of arrogant on my part, considering the shop's owner, Dan Adair, was one of the best tattoo artists around and generally was booked up weeks or even months in advance.

"Hey, Larry. Ready for what?"

"For my tat." I showed him the skull-covered helmet. "This is what I want . . . on the back of my head."

Dan smiled. "Cool. Be happy to take care of you. But you're going to have make an appointment."

"No, no, no, dude. No appointment. If I walk out of here now, I'll never get it done."

I wasn't trying to be difficult. I'm impulsive by nature, and when I want to do something, I tend to act on it right away. This is not always a good thing, of course. Sometimes a little reflection is advisable before making a decision. Tattoos often fall into that category.

"Christ, Larry, this will take all day," Dan said.

"I know, man. I'm really sorry. But I gotta do it now."

Dan sighed, walked over to the counter, and picked up the phone. He began to dial and after each call he crossed off a name in his appointment book. Within a few minutes, he was done.

"Okay," he said. "All clear for the day. Let's go."

So Dan sketched out a design based on the skull on my helmet, transferred it to a stencil, applied the stencil to the back of my head . . . and went to work. An hour passed. Constant buzzing, pressure, and what felt like a thousand little bee stings. Then a second hour. More of the same. A third hour . . . a fourth.

See, here's the thing about getting tattooed: the discomfort is not only directly related to where you are getting the tattoo—for obvious reasons, a tattoo on a meaty surface, like the biceps, hurts less than one applied to a sensitive spot with little tissue, like the head or face—but how long you will be under the gun, so to speak. The bigger and more detailed the tattoo, the longer it takes for an artist to complete his work. And as time passes, the annoying little whine of the instruments can drive you nuts, especially if it's emanating from a spot directly behind your ear. And that little stinging sensation? After a while, it starts to feel like a jackhammer.

Five hours.

Six hours.

By the end of the ordeal, my whole head was throbbing, my vision was blurry, and I felt queasy. It was like I was suffering from a massive hangover.

But what an amazing job! When he was done, after brushing off my scalp and admiring his own work, Dan spun me a round in the chair so that the back of my head faced a mirror on the wall. Then he gave me a hand-held mirror so that I could examine the results. I was awestruck. The way he brought life to the eyes. The way it really looked like a demon's face. I could almost feel its power.

"Oh, that is so sick!"

Dan smiled. "Glad you like it, Link."

By the time I left the shop, though, with my head still pounding and the image of the tat burning in my brain, pride had been replaced by concern.

Mom and Dad are going to be pissed!

It's interesting that I still cared what they would think, but I did. On some level anyway, I still wanted their approval and did not want to disappoint them. I began thinking of how I would break the news to them. I mean, it wasn't like I had just gotten a little ribbon of barbed wire on my upper arm or something. I had a huge fucking demonic skull smiling out the back of my head. Who does that—especially with their first (okay, second) tattoo?

Naturally, Mom hit me up right away; almost as soon as I walked through the door, the phone rang. She wanted to see me about something, and since I lived practically next door, there was no reason why I couldn't just pop right over. At the time, Brian Deegan and another guy named Jeff were living at my house. They were mighty impressed by the new tattoo, and they got a huge kick out of the fact that I was now all twisted up, trying to figure out how I was going to hide it or explain it to my mother.

"Fuck you guys!" I said. "Help me come up with something!"

I ended up borrowing a little sweater cap—like a beanie—from Jeff, and just pulled it down tight over my ears, so that my whole head was covered. This was not something I ordinarily did, even when my head was shaved, so it was bound to provoke curiosity from my mother. But it was the only option.

That meeting was brief, and aside from a single inquiry about whether I was coming down with a cold, the cap went virtually unnoticed. But I couldn't hide it forever. In fact, I probably couldn't for more than another day. When I talked to my girlfriend, Crystal, that evening, she told me that she had been chatting with my mother, and that we would all be having dinner together the next night. (My parents loved Crystal, by the way. Probably more than I did, and I ended up marrying the girl!)

I felt like I couldn't endure another night wearing a beanie, making small talk, wondering whether the tattoo was peeking out beneath my cap. There was still pain involved, too, which did nothing for my mood. A new tattoo feels like a bad case of road rash. It itches, it burns, it hurts. All I wanted to do was hang out at home by myself and let my scalp heal. Maybe I could do that for three or four weeks, until my hair had grown long enough to obscure the demon's features.

Or not.

Mom was suspicious from the moment Crystal and I walked through the door and kept eyeing my cap. During dinner, she finally addressed the subject.

"Larry, are you going to wear that thing all night?"

I gave a tug at the edges, pulled it down tight, so that I could barely see. I must have looked like a punk. Sure felt like one.

"Leave me alone, Mom, okay?"

"Well at least take it off while we're eating, all right?"

Then my father joined in.

"Your mother is right, Larry. Don't be rude."

Then I went into full manipulation mode, turning things back on them, laying on the guilt trip, saying I didn't feel well, asking why they were always on me to look a certain way, dress a certain way, behave in a certain way. It was an old, familiar dance in our home, although one we hadn't engaged in lately. It was also the type of behavior I'd exhibit in a major way when my drug addiction really took root. You turn the tables when someone corners you, catches you behaving badly. Instead of manning up, you try to make them feel bad.

It worked, too. Got through the whole night without taking off my cap. But my mom knew something was up. She's a pretty sharp lady and she knows me about as well as a mother can know a son. We've been through a lot over the years and she's always stood by me, helped through my various addictions and financial issues, and she's perfectly capable of seeing through my bullshit—or anyone's bullshit, for that matter. A couple days later, I saw her again, and she made some joke about the cap. Another week passed. I stopped by the house, by now confident that my sweater cap would be viewed as part of the uniform. It was a fashion statement, nothing more.

But Mom wouldn't let me off the hook.

"Larry, why are you always wearing that hat?"

I shrugged. "I don't know, Mom. It's my new thing, okay?"

And with that, she struck, reaching over as quickly as a cobra and yanking the cap off my head.

"Oh, my God!" she shouted. And then she repeated it, more slowly this time. "Oh . . . my . . . God!"

Instantly I felt bad. I tried to calm her down, but she basically spent the better part of the next half hour freaking out. I'm not sure what upset her more: the tattoo itself, or the fact that I had lied to her. Ah, let's be honest. It was probably the tattoo.

After that, there was no point trying to hide it any longer. I figured I might as well just show my dad, let him go nuts on me, and get it all out of his system. What the hell? I was a legal adult. If I wanted to shave my head and cover my skull with a scary tattoo, that was my business. Dad would have to deal with it.

"Let me see that thing," he said.

I leaned over so he could examine it closely, then waited for the onslaught that was sure to come: a barrage of insults and epithets designed to make me feel like a worthless piece of shit. But those days, apparently, were over. I remember one of the first conversations I had with my father after I started doing freestyle, a year or two earlier. He'd gotten on with his life by that point, but still openly questioned the wisdom of abandoning a potentially successful racing career to do tricks and stunts and maybe kill myself in the process.

"Why do you want to hang out with all those losers?" he had asked.

And I told him, "There are a lot more losers in the world than there are winners, Dad. Maybe I can show them something. And maybe we can all be winners."

He got it then. Or maybe a little later, after Micky Dymond and Brian Manley started showing up, and after there were movies and sponsors and journalists crawling all over the place. Anyway, he got it. So maybe I shouldn't have been surprised that he would survey the landscape of my tattooed skull, and then nod with something that looked almost like approval.

"You know what?" he said. "That's actually pretty cool."

"Really, Dad? You think so?"

"Sure. You can grow your hair out and no one will even know it's there. He gave me a little pat on the back. "Good choice."

That wasn't exactly what I had in mind, and for a number of years I went with a shaved head, just like every other rider in the Metal Mulisha. But it turned out he was right. Most of the time now, I hide the demon skull beneath shaggy hair. He's like the really dark part of my personality that can get out of control if I'm not careful. Better to keep him under wraps.

Tattoos sprouted like weeds among my buddies over the next couple years. All the guys at the tattoo shop had warned me that I'd be hooked after the first one.

"You got your ink now," they said. "You'll be back for more."

"Uh-uh," I said, scratching my scalp and remembering the pain of those six hours in the chair. "No, I won't. Fuck tattoos. I got the one I wanted. No more."

They all laughed. "Yeah, right dude. We'll see."

Sure enough, it wasn't long before I started looking at my body in different ways, thinking about myself as a canvas. I'd be sitting there at night, watching television or something, smoking some weed, and suddenly it would just pop into my head: *You know what would be really cool? A Metal Mulisha skull on my kneecap.*

A few days later, I wandered back into Soul Expression and asked Dan if he could do me that way.

"Ha! Knew you'd be back," he said.

And that was only the beginning. There were multiple trips to Soul Expression for professionally rendered tattoos up and down my left leg. And then, as I started hanging out with a rougher crowd and sunk deeper into the underworld of addiction and crime and hatred, there were buckets of ink spilled in a less-sterile manner. I have tattoos that are pretty cool; I have tattoos that cause me shame; I have tattoos that make me shake my head in wonder at how they came to be, like the one I got from the president of the Hells Angels, that carried with it a tacit understanding that I could pretty much do whatever the fuck I wanted to do.

Like I said, tattoos are a roadmap of the soul. And they do not lie.

CHAPTER 7

For a while, even after the hole in my stomach had closed and my body had healed, I kept taking the pills. And then I ran out of pills. And I had to keep asking for more, which naturally concerned the people around me. My father was the first to notice.

"I'm going to tell you right now that stuff is no good for you, and if you're not careful, you're going to get hooked on it," he said. "You really need to stop."

My doctor agreed, and shortly thereafter insisted upon beginning the weaning process. It wasn't too bad this time around. I kicked the Vicodin pretty quickly and without a lot of discomfort, but something in my brain continued to crave the drug. From that point on, I almost looked forward to getting injured so that I could get my shot of Demerol and a script for Vicodin or Hydrocodone.

Riding kept me honest and relatively clean in those days. I didn't really fall into the hardcore party scene because I was obsessed with the freestyle motocross movement. It was a fun and exciting time with so many incredible opportunities; I truly felt as though I was at the forefront of a revolution, and I didn't want to fuck it up. I was self-destructive by nature and cursed with an addictive personality, but in the early days of freestyling, there was no deterring me from the mission. Hell, I wouldn't even go to a lot of the movie premieres or the blowout parties that most guys in the scene considered to be a fringe benefit of participation in the *Crusty Demons* videos. I was dedicated and devoted to making sure that I had the best jumps that I could have, and the best freestyle facility in the world, so whenever video producers or journalists would come out to my house, I was a professional; I was the best at it. I'd learned my lesson when the kid from Spain had visited. Now I was working my ass off, perfecting new tricks, pushing the envelope farther and farther.

I wanted to be the Jeremy McGrath of the sport of freestyle motocross, or even freeriding, and to do that, I had to be more than just a novelty act. A lot of people in the motocross industry were talking a lot of trash about freestyle; they didn't show it any respect. Some of the guys on the racing circuit would occasionally dabble in freestyle because they wanted to be in the videos and keep their asses covered in the event that the sport eventually took off (it was all about brand management), but they weren't serious about it; they had no passion for it. And they were usually revealed as the amateurs that they were. I'd get so pissed off watching these guys straddle the fence that it made me even more committed. I decided that I would give 100 percent to freeriding, to become the best rider possible.

I'll admit to being at least partly motivated by the whispers in the racing community, people suggesting that the freeriders were nothing more than washed-up or untalented racers. We couldn't make a living on the track, so we turned to freestyling. I knew people would look at my outfits and crazy antics and figure I was just trying to get attention: fame for the sake of fame. They were wrong. I knew that I had to have the talent to back up the image, or I'd be nothing more than a joke. I wasn't about to let that happen. My riding had to speak for itself. I had a responsibility to myself and to the sport of freeriding, and I took that responsibility seriously.

A few people were smart enough and had the foresight to see what was happening with motocross—how freestyle had the potential to eclipse traditional racing. Steve Van Doren was one of those people.

Steve's father and uncle founded the Vans shoe company back in the 1960s. In 1995, with Steve running the company, Vans began sponsoring the Warped Tour, an alternative sports and music festival. At every stop on the tour, there were multiple stages, multiple bands, and skateboarders and BMXers performing tricks and jumps. It was a cool concept, executed brilliantly by Kevin Lyman, who had worked on the Lollapalooza tour prior to teaming up with Vans. I owe a big debt of gratitude to both of these guys for a lot of the good things that have happened in my life and career—especially Steve, who has been a friend and mentor through good times and bad. At the height of my drug addiction and madness, when every other sponsor kicked me to the curb, Steve remained steadfast and loyal. Sometimes I wonder why. But I'm grateful for his support. He's one of the good guys, for sure.

In '98 Kevin approached me about the possibility of adding freestyle motocross to the Warped Tour. I couldn't have been more stoked! But it wasn't a simple thing. You want to put on a skateboarding or BMX show, all you need is a half-pipe. A traveling FMX show is far more complicated. Logistically speaking, it's kind of a nightmare. The obvious choice for spearheading the project was Micky Dymond.

Micky was battling his own demons, but he remained one of the most creative and intense people in the sport of motocross—freestyle or traditional. Since he'd designed and helped construct all of the jumps on my course, it was only logical to seek his help in putting together a portable version for the Warped Tour. Basically, Kevin Lyman said, "How can we take the jumps from Larry's backyard and put them on the road?" Well, Micky's family owned a construction company that specialized in building custom frames for houses. One day he was at work, looking at a house truss, when he suddenly realized it could serve as an ideal base for a landing.

"All we have to do is cut it down the middle," he explained. "Make it like a big cheese wedge. It'll be perfect."

The family company was already banging these trusses out, so there were no blueprints involved. They could just crank out half-trusses. Then we brought them to my house and began setting them up as takeoffs and landings, making modifications as we went along. For a motorcycle, it's good to have some belly on the landing and some nice smooth transition so you can roll into it cleanly. The truss itself was merely a starting point. Micky and I had to go to the drawing board with these things and make changes as necessary, keeping in mind that portability was a primary concern. But we pulled it off, and that year freestyle motocross became a part of the Warped Tour.

We were on the road for nearly two months that summer, non-stop, performing at venues not only in the United States, but also in Canada and overseas. It was the first time the Warped Tour had gone international. I felt like I'd died and gone to heaven on that one. Not only was I getting to do what I loved best—riding motorcycles and entertaining crowds—but I was hanging out with musicians. I'd grown up listening to some of these bands, and now I was hanging out backstage with them. It would get even better the following year, when three of my favorite bands—Pennywise, Suicidal Tendencies, and Agnostic Front—joined the Warped Tour. These guys were the soundtrack to my adolescence, and now I was sharing meals with them in the catering tent? Fucking awesome! And most of these guys loved freestyle, as well. Thought it was about the gnarliest thing they'd ever seen. That was a trip—to be treated like rock stars . . . by rock stars.

We weren't yet making rock star money, of course, but we were doing all right. This was the first time in my life that I was earning some real cash. I was paid approximately fifty thousand dollars for that first Warped Tour, which was pretty good back then, especially for a relatively unknown guy in a brand new sport. And I got to keep almost all of it, since meals were provided and the promoters gave us a nice per diem as well. The travel was grueling and the pace relentless, but I was young and healthy and totally in love with what I was doing. I could have done two or three shows a night, no problem.

The one time I did get seriously fucked up on the Warped Tour that year produced heavy consequences. It happened in Vancouver, Canada, where some fans handed me some weed and a bag of mushrooms shortly after we got into town. I'd only taken mushrooms one other time, during a trip to Mammoth Lakes, California, about a year earlier. And on that occasion, I'd been really careful (well, as careful as you can be when you're ingesting hallucinogenic drugs bought on the street), eating a very small amount. The trip had been brief and light, nothing like the time I'd taken acid. So when this guy approached me and handed some shit in a bag, all I could say was, "Wow! Thanks, man."

"Hey, no problem, bud. You're in VC. Shit grows wild out here. Anything you want, we've got it. Enjoy!"

The weed I passed on to my buddy and fellow freestyler, Ronny Faisst, since I wasn't really into smoking at that time. The mushrooms we shared. Afterward, while waiting for the chemicals to kick in, we decided to visit a local amusement park. We were standing in line, just chillin' when suddenly I began to trip. Like acid, mushrooms work that way—you feel perfectly fine and normal one minute, and then the whole world becomes a funhouse mirror.

"Faisst, look at the head on that dude in front of us."

He laughed nervously. "No, man. Look at the guy running the ride. Look at his face!"

Mission accomplished! We got in a couple rides, experienced the semi-hilarious and semi-nauseating thrill of careening above an amusement park while tripping on mushrooms. The novelty wore off quickly, though, and we decided to just hang out and walk around while letting the drugs work their way through our systems. It wasn't a bad trip and wasn't a great trip. It was somewhere in the middle.

While walking through the park, Ronnie started telling me all about his girlfriend back home. We'd been out on the road for a while, and though there was ample opportunity for female companionship at every stop on the Warped Tour, that didn't prevent some of the guys from getting a little homesick.

"You know what, man? I really love my girlfriend," Ronnie said. "She's beautiful and sweet, and I miss her. Wish she was here right now."

"Hey, I get it, man." I said, throwing an arm around Ronnie's shoulder. "I miss my girlfriend, too. I love her. She's great."

At some point during that stupefied walk-and-talk, one of us got the great idea to call our respective girlfriends. It had been probably two or three weeks since I'd talked with Crystal, which gives you some idea of the seriousness of our relationship. I mean, it wasn't as easy to call from the road then as it is now, obviously, since cell phones were hardly ubiquitous in 1998, but if she meant that much to me, I'd have found a way. For some reason, though, at that very moment, while all fucked up on mushrooms, I felt the urge to speak with her and proclaim my everlasting love.

Or some such shit.

The next thing I knew, Ronnie and I were at a bank of pay phones, each of us cooing into the line.

"Hey, babe, I just wanted to tell you that . . . you know . . . shit! I love you! I love you so much!"

She had to have known I was fucked up, but Crystal, a nice enough girl, was more than willing to accept whatever I said. She told me she loved me, too, and that she couldn't wait until I got back home. And then, somewhere in that foggy conversation, someone brought up the idea of a long-term commitment. You know, the kind involving rings and ceremonies and legal contracts. I'm pretty sure it was me. Yeah, it was definitely me.

I remember saying, "You're the one. I'll never love anyone else as much as I love you. We should get married . . . or something."

Or something . . . would have been a better idea. But it didn't work out that way. Crystal cried and said this was the happiest day of her life.

"Me, too," I lied.

Faisst and I went our separate ways after that; I'm not sure what he did, but I went back to the tour bus and got my skateboard, because, you know, there's nothing like tearing up the half-pipe when you're tripping on 'shrooms. But I didn't leave it at that. I hopped on my board and started tearing up the street course that had been set up as well. I was just ripping it, man. Everything felt so fluid and easy. And I thought, Damn! I should eat mushrooms every time I skate. I feel so good right now.

And then it occurred to me that if I could skate this well while stoned, maybe I'd be able to surf, too.

Now that would be fuckin' gnarly!

I should have stayed focused on the matter at hand, or as focused as possible given my altered state of consciousness. Seconds later, I tried to ollie up to a little corner and grind it, but caught the wheel of my board on an edge, and just like that, I was airborne, out of control, and falling hard.

Taking a spill when you're tripping is the weirdest thing. First of all, you're not quite sure what's happened. Is it real? A dream? Is it serious? I was all alone at the time, and while the fall hurt in some abstract sort of way, I didn't sense that it was anything to get all worked up about—until I looked down and saw the gash on my arm.

Whoa . . .

It had happened so quickly, and I'd been cut so deeply, that the wound hadn't even started to bleed yet. My forearm looked a freshly filleted fish, with white meat exposed neatly beneath the skin. I could see a vein pulsating from within. I still don't know exactly what happened. Best I can figure is that I'd come down hard on a sharp edge and ripped my arm open. But seeing it like that, while fried on mushrooms, was a seriously disorienting experience. My arm felt like it belonged to someone else, like it had become detached from my body. So I picked it up, cradled it in my other hand, and set off in search of help.

We traveled with a medic (naturally), who was the wife of one of the guys on the tour. So I went back to the bus, where a bunch of people were playing dice, and found her husband.

"Hey, man, where's Laura?" I said.

"Dunno, dude. I'm winning here. What's up?"

"I fucked up my arm on the corner of the skate box," I explained. Then I held out my arm for him to see. The sight of it made him gasp, and very nearly caused me to pass out. Blood had pooled in my hand and now landed on the floor with a thick *splat!* The wound pulsated with the rhythm of my heartbeat, pumping blood everywhere. I felt sick. The truth is, I can't stand to see my own gore. I hate when I bleed. It makes me feel lightheaded and weird. I can get through the survival part of it—the pain—but then I just want to lay down and close my eyes and try not to faint.

"Okay, Larry, wait here," he said. "Sit down and I'll go find her."

Within a few minutes Laura was at my side, expertly and calmly irrigating and stitching the wound. Just sewed me up right there in the medical tent.

"Hey, Link," she said afterward. "What substance are you on right now?"

I tried to play dumb. "Huh? What do you mean?"

"Come on, Larry. Your pupils are dilated to the point where I can't see any color at all. If I'm going to treat you properly and safely, I need to know what's going on."

"Nothing . . . I'm good. Just woozy, that's all."

There was no bullshitting Laura. Not only was she a medic, but she'd spent enough time hanging out with skaters and BMXers and bikers to know when someone was high.

"Look, if Kevin finds out about this, he's not going to be happy. For one thing, you're fucked up on drugs. Second, you got hurt on drugs. Now tell me the truth."

"Okay, I ate a bunch of mushrooms and my brain is sizzling right now."

Laura laughed. "Ohhhhh, all right. Just go back in the bus and close your eyes for a while. You'll be fine. I won't tell anyone."

I think she was concerned that I was on speed or meth, or something else that might have complicated my recovery. Mushrooms, I guess, were no big deal. So Laura fixed me up and I was back out on my bike the next day. And I stayed clean for the rest of the tour.

═══════════

I came home to a wedding. Well, not an actual ceremony, but preparations were in full swing.

"Oh, my God, Larry!" my mother said. "I can't believe you and Crystal are going to get married. That's wonderful."

It wasn't like I kept in touch with everyone while I was out on the road. After that stoned call to Crystal, I pretty much just went back to work and forgot all about it. Meanwhile, though, back in Temecula, Crystal and my parents began planning for the future. I can't blame them. I mean, I put it out there. Unfortunately, I wasn't in the clearest frame of mind when I did it. I was hardly ready to settle down or get married. Sure, it was cool to talk about it; I entertained the thought that maybe, somewhere down the road, it would be nice to commit to one person, and to maybe a raise a family together. All that traditional shit. But not now. Shit, we had more chicks hanging around the freestyle scene than we knew what to do with. Hell, we had groupies, and some of them were smoking hot. I wasn't ready to give that up, not even for Crystal, who was a beautiful and thoughtful girl.

We'd met maybe six months earlier, while I was out riding in the hills one day with Nathan Fletcher and Brian Manley. We were flying back and forth over this big jump, when some other dudes rolled up and started watching us. I noticed a hot chick on the back of one guy's bike, and she just kept staring at me. Well, naturally, when that happens, you have to put on a show, so I threw it down a little harder with each successive jump, and I guess it made an impression on her. We talked for a little while afterward, and pretty soon we began hanging out.

That was Crystal.

My parents loved her from the very first meeting. She seemed like a good girl, kind of nice and wholesome, came from a good family and everything. Shit, she was raised a Jehovah's Witness, which, for some reason, made my parents like her even more. I guess they were just happy that I was spending time with someone who didn't bear the scars of the party scene. Crystal looked happy and healthy. She was . . . normal. In my parent's eyes, I'm sure she was just what I needed, especially having only recently crawled out of the gutter, where Laura and I had spent most of our time.

By the end, Laura and I were fighting more than fucking, or even getting fucked up. Friends and family members had grown accustomed to seeing Laura on the attack. She was absolutely nuts by the end, to the point where every argument invariably escalated to physical violence. Not by me—I'd never, ever hit a chick—but by Laura. She'd jump on me, start punching and scratching, kicking and gouging, cursing me out. Totally whacked. The only way that I could get her to calm down was to grab her favorite bong—expensive, hand-blown glass—and threaten to break it.

"If you don't relax, I'm going to smash this thing into a million pieces."

Usually, it worked. Sometimes it didn't.

So you can probably see how my parents considered Crystal to be a fairly significant step up in the girlfriend department. She had a job, a nice family, and she got along great with my mom. We'd been dating (if you want to call it that) for only a few weeks before she practically became a member of the Linkogle family. So when I called from the Warped Tour and talked about marriage, things sort of took on a life of their own. It didn't matter that I was fried on mushrooms at the time. I'd put it out there, and now I had to deal with the repercussions.

"Your father and I are so happy," Mom said. "She's the perfect girl for you."

"Uhhhh . . . yeah. She's awesome."

Seriously, by the time I got home, Mom and Crystal had begun talking to caterers, designing invitations, and looking for rings.

"I want her to have the same ring that your father gave me," Mom said. "It'll be so romantic."

Everyone was happy, even Crystal's family. They were all completely caught up in the excitement of planning a wedding. But I knew in my heart that it was a terrible idea for us to get married, that our relationship was completely and utterly doomed. Not because of anything Crystal had done, or any shortcomings on her part, but simply because I wasn't fully invested. My strategy, cowardly though it might have been, was to do nothing. I figured I'd just drag things out, put off decisions for a while, and eventually the whole thing would blow over. It wasn't until the invitations went out and the RSVPs started filling up the mailbox that I realized I might have made a tactical error in not addressing the matter right away.

We were married in April 1999—right around tax day! Appropriate, in some weird sort of way. I'd been putting things off and now payment was due. There was no getting around it. As the date approached, I couldn't get over the fact that everyone seemed so excited by the prospect of Crystal and me getting married. Mom was about as happy as I'd ever seen her. I'm an only child, and Crystal had become sort of like the daughter she never had. Mom is a huge Disney fan, and Crystal became like her little Snow White. They'd shop together at the Disney store. They'd go to Disneyland. They'd sit together for hours and watch Disney cartoons. It seemed like just as I was about to get up the nerve to call off the wedding, I'd see Mom and Crystal doing something together, as close as any mother could be with her future daughter-in-law, and my onions would shrivel.

Oh, fuck! All right, Larry. You can do this. You've been on the road, you've travelled, you've seen the world. You can settle down now. You can get married now. Hell, it's only, what? Fifty years? Shiiiiiiiit.

I knew it was a tragedy waiting to happen. I'd even seen my buddy Nathan make the same mistake, and hadn't learned a damn thing. He was going through a horrible divorce just as I was getting ready to walk down the aisle. But I couldn't disappoint my mom; I couldn't disappoint Crystal or her family. There were so many people involved by this point that it just seemed like too much work to back out. Idiotic, I know, but that's the way I looked at it. I just said to myself, *Fuck it, I'm going to hunker down and be a man. I'll get married and we'll do it right.*

I was totally deluded.

Here's my advice (and I'm not one who should be offering advice on much of anything, but on this particular subject, I have some painful first-hand experience): if you have doubts about getting married, call it off. Trust me, the shame and embarrassment of a cancelled wedding is nothing compared to the agony of a divorce.

There was, predictably, an epic bachelor party. I didn't really want one because I wasn't into the whole idea of getting married anyway, but all my friends, and even Crystal, insisted that we do something. The burden of arranging the party fell on Brad Palmer, who was supposed to be the best man at my wedding. In the late '80s and early '90s, Brad was the drummer in a really good death-metal band called Deeds of Flesh. When I started a band of my own, I recruited Brad to be part of it. I played bass and my friend Jeff McDermott played guitar. Our singer was a guy named Paul Duran. We called ourselves Scythe, and Brad was definitely the star of the band, the guy with the best chops and the serious music reputation. In the underground world of death metal, Brad had a cult following as one of the fastest, most aggressive guys around.

Well, two nights before the wedding, Brad got into a little trouble with the law, and I ended up having to bail him out of jail. It was a mess and it was all Brad could do to get his shit together in time for the wedding. The bachelor party understandably fell through the cracks. Or would have anyway, if some of my other friends hadn't picked up the slack.

"Bro, we have to do something for you," said Trigger Gumm.

"Yeah, man," added Nathan. "Whatever you want to do."

I thought about it for a minute or two and then said, "You know what? I just want to hang out with you guys. Let's go out in the hills and eat some acid."

Seriously, that's the way it unfolded. Seemed like a fairly benign suggestion to me, a whole lot less dangerous than drinking ourselves into oblivion and banging strippers the way guys usually do at a bachelor party. Instead we wound up in the mountains, getting fried on acid that, at first seemed to be bunk, but ultimately turned out to be incredibly clean, potent shit. I won't bore you with all the details of another psychedelic trip, especially since there was nothing particularly harrowing about it. But I remember at one point sitting in front of a fire, hallucinating that tiny lava worms were burrowing in and out of the embers. Each of us had his own little private trip, and mine centered around the lava worms, with whom I held an imaginary, but entirely honest, conversation about marriage and commitment and honesty.

"I am not ready for this."

"Sure you are. You can do it. She's a great girl. Beautiful."

"That's not the point. I don't want to get married. I don't love her. I could have saved myself a big problem by just calling the whole thing off when I got home."

"Too late now, dude. You got the tux and everything."

"Yeah . . . the tux. No turning back."

We did a rehearsal the next morning at church, and Nathan was so hungover and sick that he hurled on the altar. We'd all eaten a bunch of wild oranges the night before, and Nathan chunked them up right next to the minister's feet.

Crystal and the bridesmaids were so bummed about that. I remember feeling really shitty about the whole thing. Not just my involvement, and the fact that I knew it was a mistake, but the way we weren't giving the whole concept of marriage its proper respect. Here was Crystal's family, all her friends and sisters, a bunch of good people, and they're watching me and my rag tag group of surfers and bikers and death-metal musicians, all fucked up, still frying from the night before.

I felt bad for them and I felt bad for myself. But not so bad that I didn't go through with it. We were married that day, and for the next few months, we went through the motions of acting like a young married couple. But there was zero commitment. I would say the arc of our marriage consisted of probably three months of us actually trying to make it work, and then three months of disinterest and disillusionment. By the six-month mark, we weren't even living together anymore.

Here's the crazy thing: Crystal went directly from her parents' house to my house, and as soon as she got out from under their roof, she found some new friends and got into the party life. And when that happened it was a like a whole new world opened up for her. She was doing the kind of stuff that I'd been doing a few years earlier. So we were moving in different directions, hanging with different people, almost as soon as we got married. By the late fall, I figured our marriage was over. Crystal had moved out and was living with some of her friends. I was living someplace else and trying to focus on my riding and the expansion of the Metal Mulisha, which was beginning to evolve from a loosely connected bunch of freestyler motocross riders into a legitimate business enterprise. I didn't give Crystal or our marriage a lot of thought, until the following April, when I received a letter from her attorney, notifying me that Crystal was filing for divorce.

It happened right around our one-year anniversary, which was no accident. California has some onerous laws regarding communal property, as I was soon to discover. In California, a spouse is entitled to half the couple's net worth in the event that their union is severed following a period of at least one year. Everything gets split right down the middle—fifty-fifty. Apparently, it doesn't matter whether one spouse brought more to the marriage than the other. Unless, of course, you have the foresight to demand a prenuptial agreement, which I did not. So, one year after Crystal and I were married, I was served with divorce papers stating that my soon-to-be ex-wife wanted 50 percent of everything.

Half of the house, half of the car, half of the savings and checking accounts.

She even wanted our dog. People laugh at that, like it couldn't be true, but it was. The fucking dog was listed right there on the document, alongside the silverware and the china. And the irony of it was that her lawyer was the father of one of my friends. Not a close friend, but someone I knew pretty well; our bands used to practice together sometimes. And as we went through the process, I kept hearing Crystal's voice, and what she said when we'd first decided to get married.

"I love you, Larry, and if for any reason things don't work out, well, then they don't work out. I will never try to take anything from you."

Love is good and all, and I suppose marriage works for some people (although not for me). But it's a good idea to remember that marriage is also a legal arrangement. That was the first time I realized just how much power lawyers have; it wouldn't be the last. I was far from wealthy at that time, but I sure as hell had more money than my wife, who basically had nothing. I had a house and a car, and I was making decent money on the Warped Tour and through the *Crusty* videos; I had a few sponsors. I'd worked hard for what I had achieved and wasn't about to give it up without a battle. So I hired an attorney and fought like hell.

I remember the lawyer explaining that Crystal had claimed she'd been exposed to a lifestyle she could no longer afford, and therefore it was my responsibility to help her maintain that lifestyle.

"Dude, we were together for six months," I said in utter bewilderment. "Less than that, really."

"That's California, Larry. Sorry."

It dragged on for a while, the two of us sparring through our lawyers, before eventually settling things in relatively amicable fashion. Crystal even remained friends with my family and was working at the Briar Rose Winery as recently as last year. So that's all good. The truth is, I really couldn't blame Crystal for any of this. I should have had the balls to tell her the truth as soon as I got home from the Warped Tour.

"Babe, you're a great girl and all, but I am not marrying you."

Would have spared us both a lot of grief. Live and learn, I guess.

Or not.

CHAPTER 8

A funny thing happened to freestyle motocross in the late 1990s: it blew up. Unfortunately, in the aftermath of the explosion, it became less about creativity and freedom and riding for the pure joy of it, and more about competition and subjectivity and corporate dollars. In other words, it started to look and feel a lot like traditional motocross. As contests and sponsorships became more common, freestyle began siphoning off some of the better riders from the racing world, all eager to ride the wave of popularity and chase the money that went with it.

I was terribly conflicted about all of this. Sure, I was proud of having played an important role in the evolution of freestyle motocross; I just wasn't particularly happy with where it was going. I considered myself primarily a freerider, not a freestyle motocross competitor. And yet, it was clear that the continued growth of freestyle was going to be linked to contests and competition. I shouldn't have been surprised—the same sort of thing had happened in snowboarding and skateboarding and other action sports. In the beginning, the stars in those sports were guys who simply went out and did gnarly tricks and caught big air and made videos. But the X Games and similar competitions changed everything. The stars were the guys who could not only nail the best tricks, but who also picked up hardware at contests and knew how to manipulate and market their own brand. I could see the handwriting early, and I didn't like it.

The first national freestyle championship was held in Las Vegas in the summer of 1998, but the real coming-out party was held in November, in Memphis, Tennessee, where freestyle motocross joined the lineup of action sports at the MTV Sports and Music Festival. That event simultaneously sparked a lot of controversy and helped define the whole tone of the Metal Mulisha. We were, at that point, a fledgling business still trying to figure out how to market an attitude as well as a line of clothing. Basically we were like a team of riders in a sport that promoted only individuals, and our team motto was "We don't give a fuck!" Which wasn't quite true. We cared about freestyle motocross, and we cared about expanding the sport we helped create. But we didn't really care what people thought about us, or about pleasing sponsors. We were heavily tattooed, wrote vulgar shit on our bikes, and partied to excess.

We were the bad boys, and we knew it. And we liked it that way. Truth is, some of the smarter guys who promoted FMX competitions liked it that way, too, since it gave them an angle. Good guys (like the clean-cut teenage superstar Travis Pastrana) versus bad guys (anyone from the Metal Mulisha). And who were we? Well, me and Deegan, for starters. And Mike Metzger and Ronnie Faisst. There was Jeremy Stenberg, who was just a kid when we got to know him. He had Tourette's so we nicknamed him "Twitch." And Trigger Gumm. It was a small group in the beginning, with no clearly defined entry requirements. You had to have the right look and the right attitude. And you had to be good on a bike, of course.

We brought anarchy to a sport that was trying to get organized. We were crazy, and I was the craziest. I remember doing all right in the freestyle motocross competition at the MTV Sports and Music Festival. I finished somewhere in the top ten, and then stole the spotlight during a post-event interview with Rob Zombie, who was one of the commentators. Rob is one of the kings of heavy metal, of course. He's also proven himself to be a true artist by directing films that have been both commercial and critical achievements. Rob understands shock value, though, and he got a huge kick out of my act. I wore a chest plate on which the words "Color Me Blood Red" were spray painted. "Kill Yourself" was scrawled across my motorcycle. I suppose I should try to put that in proper perspective, but I really can't. I wasn't advocating suicide; it was all about pissing people off and demonstrating to the world that that I simply didn't care what anyone thought. They were going to take my sport and turn it into something tame and sedate? I don't think so. Not if I had anything to say about it.

Rob loved my attitude and appearance; he loved the fact that I used death metal as my accompaniment. And I think he liked the way I performed. Regardless, he became a fan.

"Man you were the best rider here," he said. "I love your whole deal."

Then there was this stoner band called Monster Magnet performing, and they were kind of hot at the time, so everyone was kissing the lead singer's ass and I started punking the dude and calling him "monster maggot" and other stupid, disrespectful shit, just to get a reaction. Some reporter from one of the motocross magazines ran tape while interviewing me, and I tried to give him an earful.

"What's up with the Metal Mulisha?" he asked. "What are you doing in your off time?"

"Well, basically, I've put together a legion of midgets that I keep locked in a basement. We have their teeth filed sharp and they're armed with trash can lids and syringes. Then they take to the streets at night."

I see some of the interviews from that time period and I have no idea what was going through my head. I wasn't really doing it for comedic effect. I wasn't even that fucked up on drugs yet. It was all about trying to make people angry. So whatever whacked-out idea came to mind, I'd throw it out there. I was frustrated by the rapid evolution of the freestyle scene. I didn't like the fact that so many people who once shit on the whole concept of freestyle were now suddenly embracing it, trying to cash in on it. Riders who flipped out when I used to do big jumps in the middle of a race, and who thought freestyle was beneath them, now wanted to be part of freestyle competitions. Big corporate sponsors wanted to throw money behind me. I was seriously ambivalent about the whole thing. My partner, though, had no such qualms. Deegan was more than happy to team up with anyone who was willing to write a check. I should have known then that our relationship was doomed. He just wanted the money, whereas I was like, *You mother-fuckers! A year ago you didn't even care if existed. And now you want me to sell your shit? Fuck you!*

At one point I was asked by a reporter if I wanted to thank any of my sponsors. At first, I said no. Then I thought about it for a moment. I'd been riding for Etnies Shoes for about a year. They were a legitimate sponsor paying me legitimate money. In fact, they were probably my biggest contract. So I thought it would be appropriate to acknowledge their support in a manner that everyone would understand and appreciate.

"I'd like to thank Etnies Shoes for giving me gear that I could trade for meth!"

Remarkably enough, no one thought that was funny, especially the suits at Etnies. They very quickly fired my ass for that one, which only served to fuel the fire of dissent. I remember getting the news that my contract had been terminated and feeling both surprised and indignant.

Really? You're firing me for that? You guys come into my world and you don't even know what I'm all about. You know that I am going to do something like this—that's the reason you hired me in the first place. That person, the one who said he was going to trade his shoes for meth? That's the guy you hired. You wanted the bad boy; you got him. And now you're going to pretend you're offended? Go fuck yourselves.

I see it somewhat differently now. I understand that there are lines you can't cross. But the truth is, I was playing exactly the role they wanted me to play.

And they didn't suffer any repercussions.

Again, I'm not trying to justify this attitude. It's immature and self-righteous and not really good for business. But that's who I was. Everything was moving too fast. I felt some of the same frustrations with freestyle that I had felt with motocross and supercross. But it was much more intense, much more personal. Freestyle motocross was like a little tomato plant that I had grown organically from a seedling. It was this baby that I had nurtured and fed and cultivated, just me and a core group of friends. It was our thing and we cared about it deeply. We didn't want it to become bastardized or exploited. Most of us didn't anyway. For the longest time, we had been bombarded and attacked from every angle. People tried to shut us down and close every door. We were a threat, and threats have to be eliminated.

And then one day, we weren't a threat. We were an opportunity. And with opportunity comes hard choices.

There were times when I tried to get control of it, but I was out of my element. And the way that corporations and bureaucracies work make it very difficult to swim against the tide. I can remember having meetings with a bunch of the guys in our sport, trying to organize everyone and get people to stand up for what they believed, and to protect the sport we had created.

"Without us they don't have an event," I said. "There are only about twenty of us in the world doing this at the highest level. If we stick together, we have leverage, because without us, they don't even have an event."

The way I saw it, freestyle was a sport we had created in part because we wanted to get away from the people who were taking all the money and making all the rules, and in a sense, exploiting the athletes, making them perform for peanuts. But freestyle grew so quickly that there was no way to maintain control or to ensure that the athletes would remain unified. It very quickly became a money grab, with each rider trying to get as much as he could, as quickly as he could.

To me, it was all about camaraderie—everyone helping each other out, pushing the limits of what we thought we could do on our bikes. For Brian Deegan it was about promotion. He enabled the promoters who wanted to pit good versus bad guy, and he was happy to have the riders in the Metal Mulisha play the part. I thought it seemed stupid and artificial, barely a step above the theatrics of professional wrestling. But Brian loved it. He thought it was a great way to grow the brand. And maybe he was right. But it kind of made me sick to my stomach, and it quickened my departure from the sport I had helped create.

═══════════

For me, the serious partying began at the 1999 X Games in San Francisco. This was a transcendent moment for freestyle motocross, the first time the sport had been included in the X Games, which of course is the showcase event for action sports. Travis Pastrana won the event and promptly rode his bike off a pier and into San Francisco Bay, a celebratory act that became the signature image of the X Games that year. I finished in sixth place, slowed by injuries and a lack of consistent training. But my mind wasn't on getting better. It was about getting away. That night I got loaded to a degree that I'd rarely experienced. There was some kid at a party who offered me a handful of painkillers, and I happily accepted. I did a few lines of cocaine. And then I started drinking Jack Daniels to come down a little bit from the coke.

And from there, I was off to the races (so to speak). Knowing what I know now about addictive personality types, I realize I was the last guy in the world who should have been messing with this stuff, because there was only one way for it to go. And that's exactly the way it went. I couldn't understand how people could use drugs or alcohol recreationally, with few apparent consequences. They'd have a beer or two, maybe smoke a joint, or hit a line of blow, and then they'd say goodnight and go home. In the morning, they'd get up and go to work. Me? Soon as I started partying I'd be worried about how soon the party might end; I had no intention of going to sleep for at least the next three or four days.

In time (and it didn't take long, really) I came to hate the sport I had created, as did some of my friends. Our contempt stemmed largely from the corporate constraints that seemed to prevail on the fast-growing freestyle circuit, but it might also have had something to do with the fact that we spent too much time partying and not enough time practicing. As a result, I routinely got my ass kicked in competitions and soon fell behind the curve. That can happen quickly in action sports. The evolution is remarkably swift, with athletes and daredevils from all over the world simultaneously pushing boundaries. You look up one moment and you can't believe someone is executing a Superman. The next thing you know they're doing backflips on their motorcycles. The bar slides forever upward, and either you rise with it or you get out of the way.

I was still one of the top freeriders in the sport, but my attitude basically sucked, and I didn't mind expressing my anger and frustration to anyone who would listen. As a result, I soon became nearly as much of an outcast as I'd been in motocross racing.

The thing is, freestyle is a judged sport—in many ways, no different than gymnastics or figure skating. Every athlete is subject to the whims of those who hand out the scores, and if you're not popular—if you start an event by riding out on the course, flipping off the judges, and flashing your appearance check— well, you're probably going to suffer. I know I did. Some of this behavior I now regret, of course, but it had the odd effect of actually increasing my popularity in some circles. I was considered an anti-hero, unwilling to conform to industry standards, unwilling to toe the line. I didn't really care about competitions anyway. Hell, that's one of the reasons I quit racing. I didn't really want to compete.

I wanted to *perform*.

My partner, on the other hand, was a much quicker study than I was, and far more adept at playing the game. Brian figured out what was acceptable and what was unacceptable, and knew how to walk right up to that line without crossing it. As a result, he became the primary face of the Metal Mulisha, and the person with whom event promoters and sponsors preferred to conduct negotiations. Sometimes I was privy to these discussions, sometimes not. I understand now that Deegan's popularity worked against me, and he knew it. He was supposedly my best friend and business partner, but he began undermining our relationship at a very early stage. I took the rap for anything that went wrong with the Metal Mulisha. If a sponsor or promoter considered something too edgy or hardcore, well that was Larry's doing. If it was smart and funky but suitable for a family audience, that was Brian's contribution. The truth is, they were often absolutely right in that assessment. But I believed passionately in what I was doing. I really was anti-establishment. I wasn't fence running. I really was opposed to much of what was happening with freestyle in the late 1990s, and I wasn't about to pretend that I was buddies with the people who were trying to get their claws into the sport. I didn't want to wear their logos. I didn't want to wear their stickers. I didn't want to be part of what they were doing.

I wanted the Metal Mulisha to be like a family—a place where young riders could grow and improve and be part of something bigger than themselves. We could make some money by selling our own gear and marketing our brand. But we'd have control over it. No selling out, no compromise. I didn't like the idea of bending over for other sponsors and behaving in a certain way and performing in freestyle contests that weren't really contests to begin with, and that were tightly controlled by some group of "officials" who were simply trying to make a quick buck. It felt too much like motocross or supercross, and I grew to hate it.

In fact, in some ways, it was even worse than motocross because of the subjective nature of freestyle competition. While the playing field in motocross racing wasn't exactly level—the riders with the best sponsors got the best equipment and support and thus were more likely to win—at least the param-

At six, jumping for the first time while in Oregon.

Reflecting on how much I hated the pressure, 1989.

Hey, tricks were limited back in 1989.

By this time I was getting over racing and throwing in tricks at the finish line.

The Bandit

WIDE OPEN

MX MAGAZINE™

Volume 1 #5

U.S. $2.95   Canada $3.95

Told you I made the cover! Photo by Flynn.

AMA San Diego Supercross in 1996.

Inked.

Catching on fire for the *Crusty Deamons Show*.

Practicing for the world record jump.

Jumping a barge in Australia.

Riding at the Mulisha compound.

Photo by Garth Milan.

Santa Barbara, 2008—Photo by Garth Milan.

Photo by Garth Milan.

eters were clearly defined: if you crossed the finish line first, you won. In freestyle motocross, the winner was selected arbitrarily by a panel of judges, some of whom had no idea what the fuck they were doing. And even if they did have some concept of the sport and the relative difficulty of various tricks, they were still human beings, and sometimes they were easily swayed. The hard truth is this: there is no such thing as a fair contest. You cannot legitimately judge something without being biased. That is true of everyone who has ever judged an event in any sport. The bias may stem from a personal connection or it may have something to do with personal preference. But it's there, and there is no denying it. Not long ago, I was asked to judge a contest, something I don't usually like to do. It was hard for me because a couple of youngsters I know were involved in the event, and I felt an instinctive need to protect them and give them better scores. I fought it; I did the best I could. But I know how difficult it is to be completely impartial.

This was especially true in the early days of freestyle motocross, when there was no standardized scoring rubric, nor any real pretense of objectivity. Judges were allowed to sit together during competitions and discuss the performances of various athletes, rather than being separated and reaching their own conclusions. Judges should never be allowed to debate the merits of a particular competitor; they are too easily swayed.

"I'll give Link a five on that run. How 'bout you?"

"No way, dude. That's a three at best."

"Yeah, maybe you're right. I'll knock him down a point."

Eventually, though, the impropriety got worse. Much, much worse. Simple favoritism, provoked by friendship or popularity, occasionally gave way to outright cheating. I'm talking about athletes offering money to judges in exchange for favorable treatment on their scorecards. I'm talking about bribes. I'm talking about riders buying medals in freestyle motocross at some of the biggest events in the sport. I saw it happen. I was there, in the room, when a well-known and successful rider offered a couple judges a significant amount of cash if they "helped" him win a medal. And they did.

At first I was amazed; maybe I was even a little impressed that anyone could pull this sort of thing off. In fairly short order, though, I got tired of it. Really, it's no different than what some high-profile athletes have done in other sports. It's cheating. The only difference is that a lot of those guys eventually got caught. Lance Armstrong was revealed as a bully and a cheat and a liar. He lost his medals and millions of fans as a result. Jose Canseco, Roger Clemens, Barry Bonds? All those guys using performance enhancing drugs in baseball? They're paying for it, too.

But freestyle motocross seemed so corrupt to me that people really didn't even have to worry about getting caught. No one gave a shit. It was almost like boxing. People were so accustomed to an uneven playing field that they didn't expect fairness. But even in boxing you could trump all the bullshit and the payoffs and the unscrupulous ass-fucking promoters by knocking out your opponent. I got the idea that the only way you could guarantee a medal in freestyle, it seemed to me, was to dig into your wallet.

After a while the corruption really began to gnaw at me. Not just because I wasn't winning, but because of what it was doing to the sport. I'd started out as a freerider, then embraced the idea of freestyle competition because I thought it would help the sport grow. And it did. But there was an awful price to pay. I trained and worked hard and tried to come up with interesting tricks in the first few years of freestyle. Sure, I acted like something of a psycho at times, but I backed it up with legitimate riding skill. So, I stopped caring about freestyle competition. If you could buy a medal, what was the point of competing? The sport had lost its innocence. It was dirty. And I really wanted no part of it.

At the same time, there were lots of guys out there who were taking it very seriously, practicing every day, trying to learn new tricks, perfecting their craft.

Whether they suspected that the sport was frequently rigged, or simply didn't give a shit, I have no idea. But I fell behind the curve pretty quickly. I still rode a lot, but I didn't *practice*. I was just having fun on my bike and trying to do new things. By the end of 1999, freestyle competitions were popping up all over the country, and guys like Deegan were becoming stars, which was good for our company, but I knew by then that I would never again be a serious freestyle competitor. It simply did not interest me.

All of this naturally begs the question of whether all action sports—skateboarding, snowboarding, BMX, etc.—are subject to the same sort of mischief when it comes to judging and competition. I don't know the answer because I don't know the politics in those sports. But it's not the same judges or the same lifestyle. It's a totally different subculture than what you'll find in freestyle motocross. Our sport attracted (and still does attract) the gnarliest guys in the action sports world. It was, and is, the Wild Wild West.

CHAPTER 9

J ump shows and videos—they were the best. You didn't have to worry about judges or corruption or anything like that. You'd just go out there and put on a good show and collect a nice paycheck. It was easy money, with little or no pressure. To me it seemed pure, real. It was all about riding and having fun and pushing yourself for the sheer hell of it. In many ways, it was no different than what we were doing back home, five years earlier, when no one was watching and no one cared. But now, suddenly, there was an audience for it, and I felt like I could do it almost on my own terms.

Australia was the best. I went there for the first time with the Warped Tour in 1998, but that was a multi-sport format, revolving primarily around music and partying. It wasn't until the following year that I came to understand just how popular freestyle had become Down Under. We went as part of something called the "All Crusted Out Tour." It wasn't really a "tour," in the traditional sense of the word. Just a couple stops in western Australia. But the response was incredible.

The tour was the brainchild of an Australian named Wayne McNabb. I'm not even sure of his background. I'd met him one year when he was backpacking across the United States. He'd fallen in love with freestyle motocross and said he had some big contacts in Australia who would be interested in organizing some jump shows. McNabb was an unusual dude, but I liked him. He seemed not to have any resources at all—no money, no car, slept in garages or tents—and yet he claimed to be connected back in Australia.

"We have to bring freestyle down there," he said. "Australia needs this. They love anything to do with motorsports. It'll be big. Trust me."

I didn't really question or give it much thought. I figured he was just talking.

"Whatever, man. If it happens, cool. I'll be there."

About six months later, out of the blue, I got a call from McNabb.

"Hey, mate. You ready?"

"For what?"

"I got it all set up. You're coming down!"

I don't know how he did it, but McNabb had teamed up with Dana Nicholson and Jon Freeman of Fleshwound Films, the guys who had created the *Crusty Demons of Dirt*, and together they had assembled the All Crusted Out Tour. I still found it kind of hard to believe that McNabb had pulled this off, but I was more than willing to take part. The fee was ridiculous: approximately thirty thousand dollars for each of two shows, along with expenses and a chance to just ride and hang out with my buddies. Brian Deegan, Mike Metzger, Carey Hart, and Seth Enslow would all be jumping, as well; Micky Dymond designed the course. By the time my plane tickets and itinerary arrived, I was stoked, even if I didn't know exactly what to expect.

The plane trip was brutal, some twenty hours in coach, with long layovers in Japan and Malaysia along the way. We arrived two days after we left, jet-lagged and disoriented. Limping through the airport, bags slung over our shoulders, we wanted simply to get to the hotel and recuperate. But as soon as we stepped outside, it was apparent that this would be a different sort of trip. Rather than taking cabs or courtesy vans to the hotel, we climbed into a waiting limousine. I hadn't been in a limo since that senior prom with Paige. And while I was generally opposed to the whole idea of motocross riders acting like superstars, I have to admit it felt pretty good at that moment. We were all kind of tripping over it.

When we pulled up to the hotel, a crowd of people were waiting outside. They waved and screamed as we got out of the limo and walked to the front door. This was like nothing any of us had ever experienced. I mean, we had fans back in the States, but they were hardcore and you almost had to go out of your way to find them. Even on the Warped Tour, I could walk around town and not be recognized. Hell, half the time I wasn't even recognized in my own hometown. This was nuts.

"Hey, Link!" I heard someone shout. "Is that you? Is that the fuckin' wombat!?"

It wasn't just me, though. They knew all of us, and they seemed particularly fond of Seth, whose infamous and horrific crash in the sand dunes in the first *Crusty* video had made him a legend among freestyle fans all over the world. Especially, as it turned out, in Australia. We were all like rock stars down there, but Seth was on a different level; people would go crazy as soon as they saw him. Simply by having survived that accident he had taken on almost godlike status.

For the first time in my life, I was exposed to a celebrity lifestyle—people wanting to be around us simply because we were famous. We had all the chicks, just beautiful women. There was champagne and drugs and parties. Frankly it was a blast. And each of the two events attracted crowds that were unthinkable for a freestyle show in the United States. Tens of thousands of people—the kind of crowd you might see once a year in traditional motocross, at the outdoor nationals. And they were all just there to see us, these five crazy guys doing tricks and covering big gaps on their motorcycles.

Who would have guessed?

It was bedlam, and we didn't really know how to handle it. At the end of the first show in Perth, Metzger went running up to the edge of the course, took off his helmet, and prepared to launch it into the crowd. The fans went wild, screaming in anticipation of a souvenir, but Metzger was just teasing. He reared back, took two big steps, like he was getting ready to heave a football, and then lowered the helmet to his side.

Ohhhhhh . . . Psych!

Then, with a big shit-eating grin on his face, he turned around and started to walk away.

Well, the Aussies weren't about to let him get away with that. They howled in protest, then charged at the barricades that separated the crowd from the course. Within a matter of seconds, hundreds of fans, maybe thousands, had shattered the barricades and started rushing at Metzger.

Holy shit!

He wisely tossed his helmet into the air and took off in a dead sprint, the angry mob (or what appeared to be an angry mob anyway) chasing after him. In reality, though, they weren't pissed at all. They loved what Mike had done—the whole "fuck off!" stance he had taken—and they just wanted to show their appreciation. They wanted to touch him. Regardless, he had no hope of getting away. The fans caught him, surrounded him, and began lifting him over their heads. Eventually they took over the entire course and mobbed all of us. I suppose from the outside it looked like a scary scene. Mobs can be unpredictable, obviously, even when they're basically just trying to demonstrate their affection. Metzger was a little shook up but quickly warmed to what was happening. Seth Enslow was totally cool with the whole thing. Deegan, meanwhile, seemed scared.

"You need to get us out of here!" he shouted to the security guards.

The cops and guards responded swiftly, grabbing us and pulling us toward the exits. I didn't really want to leave. I wouldn't say I was completely comfortable with the chaos, but I definitely felt like it would have been cool to hang out there for a while, see how things developed.

They shoved us into a van, but there was nowhere to go. The crowd was too big, too demanding. People kept pounding on the outside, chanting our names, calling for us. And as the craziness went on, I felt a surge of power. Whatever fear there might have been completely melted away. Here we were, hiding from this mob that simply wanted to express their appreciation for our craft. And I felt bad not responding to that. This was a shared experience; this was why I loved freestyle. This made it all worthwhile. Why were we hiding from the very people who had paid to see us perform?

"Let me out of this thing," I said. "I don't want to be in here. I want to be out there, with them."

Was it dangerous? Maybe. Okay, probably. Frankly, I didn't care. If they were going to be out there wrecking shit, I wanted to wreck shit with them. I threw open the door and jumped into the melee. Seth was right behind me. We walked right into the crowd and they went absolutely crazy, grabbing us, hugging us, high fiving, and chanting our names. The craziness quickly escalated, though, at least partly because the police tried to intervene. In my experience, that never works. The heavier the police presence, the more likely a crowd is to begin behaving violently. Sometimes I think it's a good idea to just let people have a good ol' rowdy, drunken time. You start leaning on them with nightsticks and cuffing people and making arrests, they tend to get pissed.

It evolved into a full-scale riot, with cars getting flipped over and set on fire. I got caught in the chaos, and after a little while I looked around and realized I was the only member of our entourage that hadn't found an exit. Somehow the rest of the guys had all taken off, leaving me behind on my own. And you know what? I could not have cared less. I was having a blast. But as the riot squad rolled in and people started getting hurt, I knew it was time to get out of there.

"Those mother-fuckers left me," I said to no one in particular. I was hanging out at the time with a couple Aussies, one of whom threw an arm around me and flashed a big toothless grin.

"Don't worry, mate. Nig Nog has got a ride right here."

"Who the fuck is Nig Nog?"

The guy smacked himself in the chest. "I'm Nig Nog."

"Oh . . ."

"Yeah, you'll love me ride, mate. Got a Ute—I'll get you right outta here."

So we walked through the crowd, through the fires and the trashcans and the cops, and made our way outside the gate and down the street to a parking lot. I figured Nig Nog would have a typical little crossover, like a Ford Falcon or a Holden, cars that never caught on in the U.S., but were wildly popular in Australia. They're like a short sedan with a truck bed.

No, no, no.

Nig Nog's car was a badass El Camino. Vintage muscle car with a jump seat and a 454 engine.

"Hop in, Wombat!"

"Dude, you gotta be kidding. This is sick."

"Yeah, I can get this baby up to two hundred twenty kilometers. You'll see."

The car was obviously Nig Nog's pride and joy. The thing was spotless, totally tricked out and refurbished. I can't imagine what it must have been worth. And here was Nig Nog, seemingly shitfaced, hopping behind the wheel and trying to make a getaway. I ended up in the middle of the front bench seat. Three other guys jumped in the truck bed. I took a look at Nig Nog and for some reason the issue of safety suddenly came to mind.

"You got a seatbelt in this thing?"

Nig Nog laughed. "Fuck, mate! You don't need no belt."

"Uh, yeah, I do, actually."

"Oh, all right."

We pulled out into traffic as I snapped the belt into place; no one else bothered. Having just completed a show, I was totally straight, which was definitely not the right state of mind for this little trip.

The guy in the front seat next to me laughed. "Hey, Nig Nog. Show him what you got."

Nig Nog gripped the wheel.

"Right . . . hang on, Wombat!"

The car jumped ahead, like a rocket, and began boning out, like all the way into the oncoming lane. I'm talking full-out *Clockwork Orange* style, with cars peeling off the other way and careening onto the shoulder or off the road completely to avoid hitting us. A chorus of horns accompanied our whole trip. And all the while Nig Nog just kept laughing. It was the strangest thing, because while I was scared to death, I also kind of enjoyed it. I mean, they were drunk, and just plain nuttier than hell, but I liked them. There was something endearing about them. They didn't seem like they wanted to hurt anyone (although obviously they could have killed everyone in the El Camino, and probably a few others, as well). They just didn't give a shit. I understood that attitude. I embraced it.

When they dropped me off at the hotel, drenched in sweat but totally energized, I shook Nig Nog's hand and jumped out of the car.

"You guys are fucking crazy," I said, shaking my head in disbelief.

They all laughed.

"You, too, mate," said Nig Nog. And then they drove off, the El Camino rumbling like a giant beast.

====

The All Crusted Out Tour, short as it was, confirmed what I already suspected: that I no longer had any interest whatsoever in the competitive aspect of Freestyle Motocross. I had seen from the inside what the sport was becoming, how the contests were evolving into something I'd neither intended nor envisioned. I had witnessed the corruption firsthand and had been permanently soured by the experience. Fortunately, as I discovered in Australia, there was another outlet for the freerider's creativity and skill, and another way to make a decent living doing something I loved.

From that moment on, I stopped training for contests and began concentrating exclusively on videos and shows. I wanted to travel the world with Jon Freeman and Dana Nicholson and the *Crusty Demons* crew, in search of the most unusual places to ride, and they made it possible. I owe those guys everything. Without them I never would have had a career in the first place. They saw value in the freestyle movement and they encouraged me and my buddies to do what we wanted to do. In return, I became a go-to guy for Fleshwound Films. Wherever and whenever they wanted to shoot, I was available and eager. I was twenty-two years old, had no day job, no timeline, no wife or kids. I had no responsibilities.

I was a man with a motorcycle and a passport waiting to be punched.

Life was pretty good.

CHAPTER 10

In the late spring of 2000, I traveled for the first time to South America, along with the Crusty Demons video crew. Our destination was Cusco, a city in southeastern Peru, near the Urubamba Valley of the Andes mountain range.

South America in general is a trip. The people are gnarly and the setting is breathtakingly beautiful. That combination can be jarring if you've never been exposed to it, which was the case for me when we pulled up in front of our hotel, accompanied by armed security guards. We'd barely finished removing our gear when a tow truck settled alongside our van. Apparently we had parked illegally, although there were no signs indicating as such.

My guess is that this was standard operating procedure, a way to fill the local coffers and profit from the tourist industry. In one way or another, everyone is on the take in South America; maybe the van driver or the hotel failed to grease the proper palms. Regardless, a spirited argument quickly ensued, with the van driver and the tow truck operator squaring off outside the hotel, screaming at each other and threatening bodily harm. Granted, I don't speak much Spanish, but I got the idea. The tow truck driver eventually went about his business, booting up the van's wheels and preparing to load the vehicle onto his flatbed. But the van driver fought him for the controls. The two of them were still going at it, wrestling for control, when we went into the hotel to check in. A few of the guys were somewhat spooked by the altercation, but I was amped. This was a place with energy and mystery. I couldn't wait to get out and explore the city and the surrounding countryside. It would be a great place to ride and shoot.

When Jon Freeman had called me about going to Peru, I was totally stoked. If I was a little farther out on the fringe than most guys, well, that was okay with Jon. I was a good and adventurous rider, always ready and eager to explore new places. In those days, at least, he could count on me for almost anything.

"Hey, Link, you ready to go on a mission?" Jon would say by way of introduction.

"Sure, dude. Where to?"

Then he'd tell me the locale and the plan, and my response would always be something along the lines of, "Yeah, I'm in. As long as you guys promise to get me out of jail, I'm cool. I'll go anywhere."

I sensed right away that this would be an interesting trip. Shortly after we arrived, the hotel gave all of us some complimentary cocoa leaf tea, ostensibly as a gesture of hospitality, but also to help us become acclimated to the altitude (the city of Cusco sits more than eleven thousand feet above sea level, so hypoxia and altitude sickness are legitimate concerns). The tea made me a little jittery and nervous, but did seem to help a bit. For reasons both practical and illicit, the cocoa plant is of immense importance to Peru and much of South America, but I didn't realize until that trip just how ubiquitous it was.

No sooner had I checked into the hotel than I was informed that a package was waiting for me. The sender was someone named *Señor Garcia*. I had never met Mr. Garcia, and I had no idea why the package was sent to me (or at least my room), but I had to admire his generosity. Back in my room, I opened the well-insulated box. Inside was a pristine mound of cocaine roughly the diameter and weight of a softball. It was so big and white that for a moment, I presumed it was fake. A practical joke, perhaps, to scare the guys from the States.

"Welcome to Peru, Americanos!"

Nope. This was the real deal. I'm not sure who arranged for its delivery, but it sure wasn't me. Let's just say we had a large crew of riders and production personnel, and some of them had obviously developed a taste for the white stuff. Hey, I'll pass no judgment on that. I wound up with a drug habit that made most everyone else look like an amateur. In those days, though, I'd yet to acquire much of a taste for cocaine. Later, when the supply had been exhausted, Mr. Garcia actually came to the hotel and made a delivery. Another ball of coke, roughly the same size.

"How much?" I asked.

"Fifty dollars."

Jesus . . . no wonder cocaine was so popular down there. This was a small mountain of coke, with a street value in the U.S. of probably ten thousand dollars. And Mr. Garcia wanted fifty bucks for it. If cocaine was your thing, going to Peru was like a trip to paradise.

Predictably, it soon became my thing, as well. I wasn't exactly a novice. I'd done cocaine before in the States, but didn't particularly care for it; the drug made me feel anxious and wired, maybe a little numb, even sick. I just didn't like the feeling of it. I was more of an opiate guy then. When you're hyperactive and intense by nature, you don't need a drug that makes you even more jittery. But the product in Peru was like nothing I'd ever experienced; it bore almost no resemblance to the cocaine I'd tried back home. This stuff I could do without feeling like my head was going to explode afterward. I'd snort a couple lines, and instead of feeling all amped up, like I wanted to get in a fight or something, I'd just feel a sense of euphoria. I could take a hit, then lie down on the bed and watch television, and for some reason the experience was pleasant. I'd do coke in North America and feel like I wanted to jump out of my own skin. Here I felt comfortable. Happy. But energized, too, if that makes any sense.

Yeah, I know, I'm making cocaine sound pretty attractive, which is never a good thing. But that's why people take drugs, right? Because it's enjoyable. The bad part—the addiction and the wrecked lives and the descent into madness that can follow—is not something you take into consideration when you're leaning over a line of coke fairly early in the game. And this shit? It was seriously addictive. You did it once and you wanted more. As soon as possible. And with each high setting you back only a few pennies, you could pretty much afford to get fucked up all the time.

It wasn't just the cocaine that was cheap and accessible. No bullshit—you could roll up to a pharmacy and get Valium or painkillers, whatever you wanted, without a prescription. It was fantastic. If you were too revved up from doing cocaine, and you wanted to sleep, you'd just take some Valium. Up and down. No big deal. Both were readily available and ridiculously cheap. In no other country had I ever experienced anything like this; nor would I experience it ever again.

Somehow, though, I managed to do some pretty good work on that trip. It was, in fact, a remarkable adventure.

The first mission began shortly after we arrived, when we went up into the hills above Cusco to shoot some footage and discovered that there would be complications and obstacles to overcome. For one thing, altitude really messes with a two-stroke motorcycle engine, so my bike kept stalling and sputtering and quitting. I don't know if it was because the fuel was too lean or too rich from the altitude, but it just wouldn't run properly. Interestingly, the only way that I could get it to run smoothly was to remove the air filter, which was basically choking the engine by limiting the amount of available oxygen.

That was problem number one.

Problem number two was a bit more complicated. It turned out that many of the places where we wanted to ride and film were considered sacred grounds and thus off-limits to outsiders in general, and film crews and motorcycles in particular. We tried to get proper permits, but there was no negotiating on this matter. If we were going to film here, we were going to have to break some rules.

"If we do this, and we get caught, we are fucked," said Jon Freeman, always the voice of reason.

"Come on, Jonny," I said. "We came all this way. Let's just get up really early in the morning and go for it."

"I'm serious," he said. "You're on the bike. You'll get the worst of it."

I wasn't worried. I wanted to give Jon the footage he needed, and if that meant riding through sacred ruins with the cops on my tail, well, then that's what I would do.

We drove into the mountains the next morning, just me and Jon and Dana; they would do the camera work themselves. The idea was to keep a low profile, shoot fast and efficiently, and then get the fuck out of there. I'd make a couple runs back and forth, hit some jumps, and then bonsai down the hill. They would shoot from a distance, with long lenses, so that they'd have a head start on the getaway. No point in putting everyone at risk.

"I'll meet you guys at the bottom of the hill or back at the hotel," I said. "Don't wait around for me."

I started the bike. It coughed and wheezed before finally lurching to life. Then I took off. Just as planned I made a couple runs, back and forth, back and forth, with the bike hiccupping and threatening to quit the whole time. The whole thing couldn't have taken more than five or ten minutes. I looked out at Jon. He gave me a thumbs up.

Sweet! We got it . . .

All of this took place near a little hillside village, with sun just beginning to peek through the morning clouds. In trying to be somewhat careful and respectful, I restricted my runs to a stretch of open ground where I had seen some kids playing soccer the previous day, when we scouted the location. I figured if it was okay to play soccer on that field, then maybe the natives wouldn't be too upset about my riding a motorcycle there.

I was wrong.

While it wasn't forbidden for humans to touch the ground or to walk on it, vehicular traffic of any kind was prohibited. And if that vehicle was a motorcycle burping along at sixty miles an hour, well . . . let's just say the locals weren't too happy.

But I was clueless. I figured if we were going to get in any trouble, it would come at the hands of the local authorities. So when I finished my last run and began riding toward the edge of the field, preparing to go back down the mountain, I wasn't particularly concerned. Then the bike started to wheeze and stutter.

Brap-brap-brap-brap . . .

And then it just died.

I was still coasting along at a pretty good pace when I noticed the first group of villagers emerging from their homes. At first I thought everything was cool, that this would be like Australia, where the locals, even if they didn't have any idea who I was, would get a huge kick out of seeing a guy on a big dirt bike. In my ignorance, I assumed they'd be pumped, though God knows why or how I reached that conclusion. To put it mildly, it was erroneous.

As the bike lurched past the village, I waved casually, trying to be friendly. They were not amused. All of a sudden, they started rushing me. Just a few of them at first, and then dozens of them, all charging and screaming at the top of their lungs. One guy came charging with a huge rock, tried to smash me in the head with it. I ducked at the last second, and the rock—more of a boulder, really—burrowed into the ground beside me. At that point, I started to get really nervous. These guys meant business. They didn't just want me off their land; they wanted to hurt me. With my bike engine failing, and the mob growing, I began kicking desperately at the ground, trying to propel the bike along as if it were a skateboard. But it wasn't, of course. A skateboard weighs maybe a couple pounds. My bike was more than three hundred pounds of steel and rubber. You couldn't just expect it to glide without some serious effort. So I pushed with everything I had, until finally I reached the small road that would take me back to the city. But as I coasted along, the mob kept growing, and the rocks kept flying.

These people are going to tear me limb from limb!

Finally the road began to edge downward. My speed increased. As did the size of the mob and their apparent resolve to punish me for having trespassed on their land. The road kept getting steeper and steeper, and as it did, more people kept popping out of little roadside huts, shouting in Spanish, waving their fists, tossing rocks and other debris. Now they weren't just giving chase; they were running alongside me.

It went on like that for perhaps a quarter of a mile, until the grade became steep enough for the bike to really pick up some speed, and the mob began to peel away. I put my head down and tried to negotiate the turns without braking; I didn't want to do anything that would impede my progress and give them a chance to catch up. When I reached the bottom of the hill and coasted into the city, relief was quickly replaced by uncertainty. I realized that I had no idea how to get back to the hotel. Jon and Dana had taken another route down, so I was entirely on my own.

So now I was in the center of Cusco, wandering around, paranoid and lost. All I could think about was the mob on the hillside, and how they were probably still giving chase, and that they were no more than five minutes behind me. It was a fairly long road, but if they had acquired a car or some bicycles along the route, they'd be on me soon. And when they got to the bottom, they'd find no shortage of locals willing to join the lynch mob. I would be viewed as not just an arrogant American, but someone who had committed blasphemy. They would kill me, and no one would care.

I spotted a Dumpster behind a building, surrounded by bags of trash and empty boxes. By now my bike had come back to life, so I cruised on over to the Dumpster, turned off the engine, and laid the bike on its side. Then I removed my helmet and pads, placed them on top of the bike, and covered the whole package with a bunch of cardboard. The goal, obviously, was to blend in; to not look like guy who had been riding a motorcycle. I typically did not wear riding gear, just regular street clothes, so that was a bonus. Unfortunately, as I started to walk away, I remembered something.

Fuck! I don't have any shoes!

Here I was, walking through Cusco in big, heavy riding boots. A dead fucking giveaway. I started to panic. I envisioned the angry mob pouring into the streets behind me, banging on doors, asking if anyone had seen the American biker. I pulled off my shirt, tossed it into the trash as well. And my boots. I hid everything, then walked around the side of the building into a little outdoor market where street vendors were selling all kinds of trinkets and shit. Luckily, I was somewhat prepared. See, whenever I was riding in a foreign country (actually, this holds true even today), I carried a bunch of cash in my sock, just in case I got in trouble and needed to pay off a cop or a local judge, or whomever. You never knew when you might get in trouble, and who would have their hand out. So I pulled out the cash and started looking for some cheap stuff to disguise myself. I couldn't find any shoes, but I did buy a thick pair of wool socks with the word CUSCO on the ankle. Better than the flimsy cotton socks I'd been wearing under my boots. Better than going barefoot, that's for sure. I picked up a little alpaca jacket, too, and then headed off in search of my hotel.

But that was no easy task. I had no cell phone and couldn't even remember the name or address of the hotel. And I spoke virtually no Spanish. I wound up wandering through the streets of Cusco for probably a good two or three hours, looking for something recognizable. Eventually I remembered that the hotel was located next to a park. So I stopped a few people, did my best to describe the park and ask for directions. It took a while, but finally I found a guy who could speak English and knew what I was talking about. I arrived at the hotel around noon. The Crusty guys were all hanging out in the lobby when I walked in.

"Dude, what happened to you?"

"You guys have no idea what I just went through. My bike died. Shit, I almost died! Did you see them throwing rocks at my head?"

Jon laughed. "No, man. We thought you just killed your motor so no one would hear you."

I told them the whole story, including the part about hiding my bike and my gear near a Dumpster in town.

"We have to get it," I said. "Before someone hauls it away."

So we hopped in the car with a private driver who knew the city well, and drove around for a while. I kept describing various landmarks, and he somehow got us back to the neighborhood where I'd hidden the bike. Luckily, it was still there. Mission accomplished.

After that, we were all pumped about the trip and psyched to gather more footage in places where no bike had been before. Like the Inca Trail. We drove out one morning into the middle of the desert. I rode for hours through beautiful, humongous sand dunes. And then someone suggested we get a quick shot of me riding through the Nazca Lines.

"Oh, no. Fuck that!" I said.

The Nazca Lines are one of those inexplicable ancient mysteries you just don't want to fuck with. Like the Egyptian pyramids, their existence is hard to comprehend. The lines are exactly that: a series of shallow trenches in the Nazca desert that depict designs of varying degrees of complexity. Some are merely geometric shapes; others are clearly meant to look like specific creatures: a monkey, a spider, a shark. These things are fucking huge and beautiful, but identifiable mainly from altitude. The detail is incredible, especially when you consider they were supposedly created by unsophisticated natives more than fifteen hundred years ago. How or why they accomplished this task is anyone's guess. But it's a seriously impressive and spiritual place, one treasured by the Peruvian people. You treat it with reverence, or you risk getting fucked up not only by the local authorities, but by a lifetime of bad karma.

"I've seen this shit on the Discovery Channel," I protested. "I am not riding through the Nazca Lines. You're not even allowed to walk out there. I'll get killed."

We settled for something safer and saner, but still pretty dynamic. Since we had to take a plane to get out there, we decided to get an aerial shot of me hauling ass on a highway that runs parallel to the Nazca Lines. It ended up being an amazing shot, despite the fact that I wasn't doing anything special, just leaning over the bike, riding as fast I could, parallel to the Lines. The point was simply to capture the moment, the beauty of a motorcycle racing alongside this ancient mystery. I still get a charge when I see that footage. I mean, how many people can say they rode a dirt bike by the Nazca Lines?

I don't know the answer, but I'm sure it's a small number.

Even smaller is the number of people of people who have ridden a dirt bike through the ancient Inca religious site of Machu Picchu. In late June 2000, when we were at the tail end of our trip to Peru, I'm pretty sure that number was zero. But we wanted to change that.

"I want to go here," Jon Freeman said, flashing a photo of Machu Picchu.

I knew little about the place, but the picture was undeniably beautiful: reconstructed remnants of a mountainside city built at the height of the Incan Empire, probably sometime in the fifteenth century. The more I read about it, the more I wanted to visit. Riding along the Nazca Lines was cool, but Machu Picchu was uniquely unattainable. If we could ride through Machu Picchu, that would be legit. That would be a game-changer.

"What do you think? Jon asked.

"Dude . . . I am in!"

By this time, the Crusty crew had begun to disperse. We were closing in on summer, and a lot of people wanted to get back home before the Fourth of

July. By the time we committed to shooting at Machu Picchu, there were only two of us left: me and Jon. We hired a security guard (who doubled as a translator) to make the trip with us. He traveled by train with my bike, all the way up to Machu Picchu, which was located about fifty miles northwest of Cusco, at an altitude of roughly eight thousand feet. High enough to provide gorgeous, sweeping vistas, but not so high that the bike would operate inefficiently. So Jon and I flew in by helicopter and waited for the bike to arrive.

I found Machu Picchu to be an amazing and spiritual place. You stand there and look out over the ruins and you can't help but question your whole existence. It seemed impossible to me that the Incans, without benefit of modern technology or machinery, had built Machu Picchu five centuries earlier. It was much too advanced. I couldn't shake the notion that they must have had help from some advanced form of civilization. How else to explain the detail and the precision—the fact that some of the rocks used to build the ruins were not native to the region, but rather more common some three canyons away? How could fifteenth-century humans have tackled such an enormous task?

Aliens? Maybe. Who the fuck knows? Everything was too perfect and precise. I started thinking about a trip to Stockton I'd made a few years earlier with Nathan Fletcher, when we'd both seen some strange light in the sky that hovered overhead for minutes before blazing across the sky at what seemed like warp speed, and then disappearing in a heartbeat. I'd always wondered about that one. And now I wondered even more.

It was all mind-boggling; rather than being freaked out by the weirdness of it, though, I embraced it. I suppose it might sound strange that I wanted to ride my bike through Machu Picchu if I was so intimidated by the place, but I actually thought it was neat way to express my respect. And, of course, I wanted to do something no one else had done. It helped, too, that I was doing a serious amount of coke by this time. That seemed to intensify my reaction, and my connection to the surroundings.

Jon and I scouted out the location for a while before filming. We came up with all these great angles and ideas. We needed a more detailed plan of attack. Machu Picchu is a popular tourist destination, which meant we'd have to get by some serious security in order to film among the ruins. There were two ways to do this: 1) sneak in or 2) bribe the guards. In keeping with South American tradition, we chose option number two. We wound up getting a local guide named Cucho who spoke English as well as the native dialect. Jon asked Cucho to speak with one of the security guards about what we wanted to do. It was understood, obviously, that motorcycles were prohibited; we were willing to pay to have that ban temporarily lifted.

So Cucho delivered the message to the guard. He nodded, and the deal was executed. A short time later, we began filming. As Jon worked the camera, I made one pass through the ruins. Then a second. On my third pass, a park ranger—essentially a legitimate cop—arrived on the scene. He jumped out of his car and began waving his arms furiously and shouting at us in Spanish. Totally freaking out. He slapped the face of the security guard who had given us permission—literally just smacked the guy, knocking him backwards—and then marched toward us. As the ranger yelled, Cucho did his best to translate.

"He's very upset."

Really? You think so? Don't need a translator for that.

"He says you are not supposed to be here. It's very bad."

"Tell him we paid the security guard, and that he said it was okay," said Freeman, figuring honesty was the most prudent course of action.

Cucho delivered the message. The ranger grew angrier. He kept shouting and pointing his finger, first at us, and then at the ruins.

"He says he is going to arrest you," Cucho explained.

Jon shrugged, smiled. "Well, if he's going to arrest us, he might as well let us get the last shot, right?"

This was a ballsy move on Freeman's part. The ranger looked like a tough little hombre, right down to the mustache and the bandito belt around his waist, with a couple dozen rounds of ammunition and a revolver on each hip. I did not doubt that he was willing to use them. Jon seemed unfazed. He was amazing that way; he never got flustered, no matter how gnarly the situation. Through Cucho he offered to pay the ranger more money. The ranger refused. We were going to be arrested, he said, and there was nothing that would change his mind. So Jon repeated his request to finish filming. He said it politely. With a smile.

No dice.

"Get the hell out of here," Jon said. "Let me handle this."

I did as I was told. Hit the throttle and dashed back down the mountain, leaving Jon and Cucho standing there with the ranger. I glanced back and saw the three of them getting into the ranger's car.

Although I wasn't going to jail, my situation was also problematic. I was stuck in some tiny village in the Andes, with a dirt bike and a few bucks in my sock. We had agreed to meet at the train station in the village, so I hung out and tried to blend in as best I could. But sitting there at the station, looking about as foreign as possible, and knowing that my partner and translator had been arrested, I started to feel really paranoid. It didn't help matters any that I was ripped on cocaine. It felt like everyone was staring at me, which they were, of course, but they probably meant no harm. They were just curious. But I couldn't handle it. I felt like I wanted to jump out of my skin. I ended up doing the same thing I had done in Cusco: hiding the bike beneath a mound of trash and ditching most of my gear in a feeble attempt to deflect interest. Three hours passed. I started to freak out. This was the Peruvian hinterlands, after all, and people did just sometimes disappear.

Forever.

I was trying to plan my next move when Jon walked into the station, smiling casually, like nothing had happened.

"What happened?" I said. "I was worried you weren't coming back."

Jon shrugged. "We came to an agreement."

I never figured out exactly how expensive an agreement it was, but somehow Jon got out of there. We ended up staying in Peru for another two weeks, getting more footage, this time with the approval of the local police and rangers (with the understanding that we would keep a respectful distance from the ruins).

Meanwhile, I dove into drugs in a major way. As I said, cocaine had never been my drug of choice, but the stuff in Peru was so good and so pure that I quickly developed a taste for it. Until that trip I don't think I realized just how severe an addictive personality I had. I couldn't get enough coke, and with the reduced workload and smaller production crew, there was plenty of time and opportunity.

There were a number of lost days and crazy adventures, but the most memorable involved a midnight trip to some catacombs. We were led there by a local guide named Luis, who seemed a bit nervous about the whole trip, but obliged anyway. He was getting paid, after all. Since it was after hours, we had to sneak in. We wandered around the catacombs, looking at the ancient carcasses and mummified corpses. Some of the mummies rested alone; others were surrounded by skulls. And each of the skulls had some sort of damage—usually a single hole. I didn't know what to make of it, and Luis had no idea. Eventually a caretaker showed up and chastised us for sneaking in. I guess he thought we were grave robbers or something. With Luis acting as our translator, we convinced the caretaker that we meant no harm, and he calmed down. He also explained that the mummies had been warriors, and the skulls represented the number of kills they had achieved in battle.

Pretty cool.

On the way back to the hotel, Luis reached into his pocket.

"Look what I've got," he said.

And with that he held up a small human bone.

"Are you shitting me?!" I said. "You stole a bone from the catacombs?"

Luis nodded proudly.

"Dude, we gotta go throw that thing back. I don't even want to be in the same car with you."

Luis laughed. "I'm gonna make a necklace with it!"

The next day—I shit you not—Luis fell gravely ill with some sort of weird infection. He was bedridden with a raging fever for four days before the paramedics finally took him out of there. He spent the next two months in the hospital, recovering.

That whole thing tripped me out for a long time, made me wonder about the consequences of our actions. Riding a bike across Machu Picchu is one thing. But stealing from corpses in an ancient burial ground is another thing altogether. Even in my coked-out state, I understood the difference.

You don't fuck with the gods like that.

CHAPTER 11

Whe I left Peru, I also left behind my taste for cocaine. Not so much because I was worried about its effects or whether it was ruining my life, but simply because the quality of Peruvian coke had spoiled me for anything else. But something had happened, some fundamental change in my brain chemistry and personality. I don't really know how else to explain it, but when I got back to the United States, I pretty much went off the rails.

I won't ever blame anyone else for my own flaws or mistakes, but there is no question that I was influenced by an ever-changing circle of friends. I was drawn to the craziest people I could find, self-destructive and anarchic mother fuckers who thrived on chaos and hate. Back in those days the Metal Mulisha had begun to take off as a business entity, and I don't doubt that part of its popularity stemmed from the notion that there were a fair number of "thug" types who were at least peripherally involved in our organization. We sponsored riders and eventually sponsored mixed martial artists, and some of the guys who became associated with our team were legitimately scary, if not downright nuts.

Phil Ensminger fell into the latter category. We'd gotten to know each other around 2000, when I started working out at a local gym where Phil and some other guys trained. He was a fighter who called himself "The Great White Nightmare," which had less to do with his ability in the cage than it did with his general outlook on life. Phil and I were very close friends for a while, but it was a mutually destructive relationship, as both of us were battling all kinds of problems; we were both addicts and we were both filled with inexplicable rage and hate. I still can't exactly pinpoint the root of my issues (although I suppose you could focus on my bizarre, itinerant childhood), but Phil's were fairly easy to trace.

Phil had grown up in the Pacific Northwest, joined the Marines, and then settled in Southern California, where he pursued a career in mixed martial arts. He was devoted to training and legitimately seemed to enjoy fighting (not just hitting, but getting hit). It was pretty clear that he carried some baggage, and if you listened to him tell stories about his service, and if you could presume those stories to be accurate, it wasn't hard to understand why he was scarred.

At some point in his military career, Phil said he had been involved in a hostage rescue situation in South America. He and some other guys from his unit had broken down a door while trying to extricate the hostage, and as they charged into the building, "Some little fucker was sitting there waiting for us with a sawed-off shotgun," Phil recalled. "Just hanging out with the barrel pointing right at us. Blew my friend's head clean off. His brains were in my mouth."

Phil never cried or even got particularly emotional when he told this story. He'd just sort of tell it matter-of-factly, as if it were the kind of thing that might happen to anyone. And then he'd talk about how he basically lost his mind in the aftermath of the shooting and went on a bit of a killing spree, pumping rounds into everyone in the building, "Firing so hard and fast that I almost melted the gun. I was on full auto, just kept grabbing clips until the barrel bent."

Then he'd finger the mangled dog tags that he still wore around his neck.

"That's a bullet hole from a three-round burst out of an M-14. I was lucky I was wearing my flak jacket."

Phil said he left the Marines shortly after that incident. He'd served his time and I suppose he was a little too unpredictable to keep in uniform. Every year around the anniversary of his friend's death, Phil would claim that he suffered for several days from a persistent sensation of tasting metal and iron in his mouth.

"The taste of my buddy's brains."

My dad loved Phil, partly because they were both veterans, but also because my father knew all about post-traumatic stress disorder, and how it could totally fuck up your life. Maybe he recognized in Phil some of the same demons he had fought within himself.

As for me, well, I could relate to Phil on multiple levels. Granted, I was a few years younger and had never served in the military or been through anything quite as traumatic as Phil had experienced, but there was something about the guy's intensity that resonated with me. He was way out there, always on the verge of blowing up. I mean, this was a violent, hostile guy, which, I suppose, is one reason he was drawn to cage fighting. But I always got the sense that he truly did not give a fuck about anything, including whether he lived or died. (Indeed, he would succumb to a drug overdose a few years down the road).

So back in the beginning, Phil really set the tempo for the Metal Mulisha image, because he was so loose and crazy, and his friends were scrappy, nasty dudes. These were not your average, everyday tough guys. These were guys who were way out on the fringe. They partied like crazy and they fought (sometimes with other groups they didn't like, sometimes in backyards, amongst themselves, just for the hell of it). They were thickly muscled men with shaved heads and tattoos, some of which proclaimed the superiority of the Caucasian race. This was the beginning of a period in which I hung out with some of the strangest and most unsavory characters you can imagine: racial separatists if not outright supremacists; gang members and pseudo-gang members, guys who weren't quite in the Aryan Brotherhood or Hells Angels, but perhaps aspired to get there someday.

Phil had no such aspirations; his goal was to be an MMA champion. Short (maybe five foot eight) but wide and muscular (he weighed close to two hundred pounds), Phil was every bit as dangerous and violent as the legitimate criminals who sometimes hung out with us. And as his stage name indicated, he was proud of his ethnicity. Eventually I was drawn into that circle; I allowed it to happen. In the beginning, though, I simply liked hanging out with Phil because he was dangerous and violent and angry.

Sometimes I'd stay at Phil's place out in Rainbow, south of Temecula. He lived in a little barn, almost a shack, out in the hills, in a fairly remote area known for being a popular route among undocumented aliens trying to sneak into the country. Their presence near his property seemed to both energize and infuriate Phil; sometimes I think he lived out there just so he'd have a battle to fight. He kept an assortment of guns and had drilled a small hole in the front door—just large enough for the barrel of a carbine rifle. Phil worked construction and used to leave equipment and supplies around his property; the guns, he said, were to protect his business interests.

"Fuckin' Mexicans!" he'd say. "Always stealing my shit."

I remember one night I was sleeping on the couch when Phil came flying down the stairs, grabbed the carbine and a Maglight, threw open the door, and began scanning the hillside. I stood just behind him, looking over his shoulder. Off in the distance, under the moonlight, I could see a flurry of activity, silhouettes of a half dozen people scampering away.

"I fucking knew it!" Phil shouted. He shouldered his rifle, took aim, and began pumping rounds into the desert sky. "You'd better run, assholes!"

Far as I know, he didn't hit anyone, but not for lack of effort. After a couple minutes, he lowered the rifle and closed the door.

"Mother fuckers keep coming through here. They ought to know better by now."

I remember standing there, looking at Phil, his eyes fixed in an almost psychotic glare, and thinking not that this was someone I should avoid, but someone I understood and even admired. In part this was because I'd begun to descend fairly deep into the rabbit hole, in terms of drug abuse. Through Phil and his MMA buddies, I was introduced to the magic of anabolic steroids, which not only added bulk and strength to my frame, but wreaked havoc on my fragile psyche. I was already an anxious guy with a lot of pent-up rage; steroids naturally (or unnaturally) exacerbated that condition. And the weird thing is, I knew it, and I took them anyway. A lot of athletes use performance-enhancing drugs to increase speed and stamina and strength, or to assist with recovery from injuries. They're effective, which is why people take them. They're an occupational tool. Of course they're also an occupational hazard, fraught with all kinds of potential side effects. Not that I gave a shit. I took steroids not because I thought they'd help me become a better rider, but because I wanted to be meaner and tougher and stronger. I was crazy and wanted to be even crazier. In that regard, steroids totally worked.

Phil and I had an interesting friendship. We were both drug addicts with a shaky grip on sanity, but over the arc of our relationship, he would also act like my big brother, offering advice and recommending moderation, even as he fell deeper into addiction and bad behavior himself. It was like he didn't want me to suffer some of the pain he'd already experienced. It was Phil who introduced me to a shady Orange County physician we referred to simply as "Dr. Kevorkian," because of his willingness to prescribe ("peddle" might be a better word) narcotics, specifically painkillers, to virtually anyone who walked into his office.

"Careful with this guy," Phil warned. "He's dangerous."

Of course, Phil was one of Dr. Kevorkian's patients (or customers), as well. But I quickly surpassed Phil in consumption and became one of Dr. K's favorite clients. I went to Kevorkian first to get Vicodin. Then he turned me onto Norco, a mix of acetaminophen and hydrocodone; and finally the really serious stuff—Demerol and morphine. Over the course of a year I became a full-blown opiate addict, gulping pills and injecting drugs intramuscularly.

Dr. Kevorkian also had a regular and semi-legitimate practice, but he was one of the weirdest and most unscrupulous doctors you'd ever hope to find. He gave me whatever I wanted, and I always paid in cash. He had a practice specializing in pain management and "wellness," and after a while I was invited to access the physical therapy facilities.

"Come in here," he said one day, guiding me down a hallway and into a back room, where a gorgeous young woman stood sentry over some massage tables and weights and other light equipment.

"Nice, huh?" Dr. K said. "She just got new boobs, too. Show him, honey."

And with that the hot young "physical therapist" lifted her shirt, smiled perkily, and jiggled her perfect breasts.

"Impressive," I said.

"I know, right? She'll get the kinks out for you."

"For sure."

"Just let me know if you're interested and we'll set up an appointment."

I thanked him for the offer but never partook of the service. I was there for drugs, not a happy ending.

On any given day, I could walk out of Kevorkian's office with prescriptions for Demerol and Norco, sometimes even steroids, and a bagful of syringes. Cocaine and occasionally methamphetamine I could get practically anywhere. I was hell bent for leather. Six months earlier I'd been in Peru, having the time of my life, doing some of the most memorable filming and riding of my career, and now I was falling apart. When I showed up in Australia in 2001, for a stop on the Crusty Demons World Tour, I was in no shape to ride. In fact, I'd barely ridden at all in the previous six months, having spent most of my time feeding my addiction and watching my life go down the toilet. So in love with freestyle motocross was Australia that I could get away with almost anything. Eventually, though, there came a reckoning.

I don't know whether I was arrogant or clueless, or maybe just too drug-addled to give a shit, but I basically went to Australia with enough drugs to last a normal person the better part of a year. Of course a normal person wouldn't combine Demerol, Norco, Vicodin, steroids, and coke. A normal person wouldn't pull out a syringe and shoot up in the middle of an airport. That's crazy-ass junkie behavior. And that's what I was: a junkie. A drug addict. I didn't expect to get in trouble, didn't particularly care who saw me getting high, or who was around me when I was fucked up. I even had Dr. Kevorkian write me prescriptions and an explanatory note saying I was going overseas and needed my dope. For a price, he was only too happy to oblige.

Everyone knew I was mess: my friends and family; the guys on the Crusty Tour. But no one talked about it. No one confronted me. Not at that point. They were letting me run wild, refusing to acknowledge the elephant in the room. I'm not saying it was their responsibility; it was my problem, my fault. You can't help a drug addict until he's willing to help himself, and I was nowhere near that point.

By the time we arrived in Australia, I was gone, baby, gone. I can remember being at dinner one night and zoning out while everyone else had a few glasses of wine and a good meal and tried to have fun. I just wanted to get the fuck out of there and get high. So I reached into my backpack, withdrew a loaded syringe—I was always prepared, always thinking about the next fix—and pumped a load of Demerol into my biceps. I can still see the look on Jon Freeman's face as I shot up.

Dude?! What the fuck, man?!

The freestyle motocross world, especially in those days, was a pretty gnarly place. A lot of guys were into drugs and generally risky behavior. That was the personality type that was attracted to the sport, and a live-and-let-live attitude prevailed. But even by the fairly generous standards of freestyle, I was extreme. No, check that. I was close to psychotic.

As usual, Deegan and I shared a room on that trip. He was partying, too, but I was in a totally different league. My life at that time revolved entirely around the pursuit of narcotics, as it does for any drug addict. Nothing else really matters beyond finding the next fix. And not just because you want to get loaded. I knew that if I didn't have my painkillers, I'd quickly start feeling the horrible effects of withdrawal. So when I went overseas I always made sure that my contract included a clause stipulating the need for a personal physician, someone who would be at my disposal throughout the event. I always took stuff with me, but there was no way to legally carry enough to last the duration of a trip like the Crusty Tour. I was going to be in Australia for the better part of a month, the way I was using, I had enough to last a week—maybe two weeks if I was willing to cut back and endure some low-level nausea and discomfort.

I wasn't willing.

So I needed a personal assistant, someone who could help me get whatever I wanted, whenever I wanted it. Before we left, I had a meeting with someone who told me he would be able to help me out overseas. If I said I wanted fifty tabs of ecstasy, ten sheets of acid, and enough Demerol to last a week, it would be taken care of. No argument, no debate, no intervention. If that's what I needed (if that's what anyone needed, or wanted) to get through the tour, then that's what I would have.

The intermediary in all of this was a doctor—or someone posing as a doctor—who would show up at our hotel in Sydney. He was a very dignified little man, with dark hair and glasses. Well-dressed, soft-spoken. I remember thinking the first time I saw him that he looked and carried himself more like an attorney than a physician (or a drug dealer). He carried with him a little black briefcase. I was lying on my bed, already feeling a little sick because I was running low on opiates and trying to stretch out the supply. The doctor opened the bag, revealing a veritable a pharmacopeia of vials: Demerol, morphine . . . all kinds of stuff, ready to lock and load. A real Felix the Cat bag of tricks.

"Will this work?" he asked with a smile?

"As a matter of fact . . . yes."

I had him give me a shot, and instantly I began to feel better. So much better, in fact, that I ended up destroying my hotel room, like literally ripping it apart for the sheer hell of it. I was so jacked up that I started bouncing off the walls, like I was on cocaine or meth instead of Demerol. I had all this energy and didn't know what to do with it. Instead of going outside and practicing for the show, I went on a demolition binge, rock-star style: throwing couches off the balcony into the pool, smashing windows and mirrors and television sets, and generally behaving like a narcissistic fool. Understandably, no one was very happy with me after that incident. But I was given a long leash because I had a reputation for being able to perform despite the occasional psychotic episode. Instead of imme- diately getting tossed off the Crusty Tour and out of the hotel, I was given a stern warning and a different room. This time they gave me a single—I was so out of control that not even Deegan was willing to room with me.

I look back on that tour and it's almost like an out-of-body experience, like it wasn't really me doing all this crazy shit. But of course it was me. And I have no one to blame, and no real explanation for any of it, other than the fact that I was completely out of my mind.

I remember a couple days prior to the event when a bunch of us were all hanging out by the pool. We were all watching a group of hot chicks, speculat- ing on whether they might be freestyle fans, formulating a plan of introduction, when one of the girls got up from her chair to leave. As she started to walk away, a syringe fell out of her shorts and clattered on the concrete. She walked away without even noticing, while the rest of us stood there staring.

One of the guys in our group called out to her, "Hey, you dropped some- thing."

The girl stopped, turned around, and doubled back. As she bent over to pick up the syringe, she smiled and said, "Thanks." Then she walked away.

Everyone else started tripping, freaking out that such a beautiful girl would be walking around with a syringe in her pocket. They'd been fantasizing about this chick, and now it seemed as though she was a hard-core drug user, and thus probably a girl to avoid, for any number of reasons.

Me? I was intrigued.

Whoa, not only is she hot, but she's got her own gear. I wonder what room she's in. I'll bet we could get into some really good shit together.

Some of this I expressed to the other guys, who looked at me like I was insane. Not that it registered much. I was too far gone to care what anyone thought about my behavior or what they expected of me. My focus was on one thing and one thing only: getting more drugs.

Eventually I tried a few practice runs, but I was all kinds of fucked up, so there was no way I could hit any of my jumps. I was stale and out of shape, and now I was loaded, as well. Even in my altered state of consciousness, I knew that there was no way I could take part in a freestyle show the next day. But I couldn't just withdraw. I needed a legitimate excuse, like an injury.

The thing is, freestylers ride hurt all the time. I'd done it my whole career. It's part of the game. So if you're going to beg off, you'd better have a legitimate excuse, something harsh and obvious enough to provoke sympathy, rather than resentment.

What to do . . . what to do . . . Wait a minute. I've got it. Toenail!

It seemed to make sense at the time. So I found a pair of pliers and ripped the nail off my big toe. I figured it would be one of those injuries that would look a lot worse than it actually was: plenty of blood and bruising, but not really all that bad. Well, I was right about the blood and bruising, but it actually hurt like hell. Regardless, it did the trick.

"Jesus, Link," the event director said when he saw the wound. "What the hell happened to you?"

"Ah, shit, man. I was running out of my room and I accidentally kicked the door. Total fluke. Sheered off the nail and busted my toe."

I paused for dramatic effect.

"I'll be okay, but I don't think I can ride. I'm really sorry."

"No, no, no. Don't worry about it. You just take care of yourself."

And with that act of self-mutilation, I effectively stepped off the money train. All I had to do was stay on board and collect hundreds of thousands of dollars by doing what I loved best, and what I was good at—riding bikes—but I decided to jump off and go the other way. Maybe it was just too easy. More likely it was the drugs. It wasn't like I made a thoughtful, reasoned decision. I hadn't been riding and I didn't tell anybody I hadn't been riding. I was too busy partying. So I needed an out.

Prior to the show I decided to run my bike up the landing ramp and just launch it into the air (without me on it, of course). A big, showy act of destruction that would incite the crowd and give them the impression that I'd be taking part in the regular event. Unfortunately, I was too fucked up to realize that another rider, my buddy Mike Jones, was warming up at the same time. My bike wound up hitting the bottom of his bike while he was airborne. The crowd, mistakenly thinking we'd planned the entire stunt, went absolutely nuts. But Mike was clueless. He crashed to the ground, somehow emerged unscathed, and soaked up the applause.

"Holy shit," he said. "That was incredible."

Mike wasn't nearly as pissed off as he should have been; he was a total wild man who took all kinds of crazy chances. I guess he figured it was part of the show. But the truth is, I really regret that one, because he could have been seriously hurt. A lot of people could have been hurt by some of the things I did in those days.

Near the end of the Sydney event, I was handed a microphone and given the opportunity to address the crowd. I'm not sure why anyone thought this was a good idea—probably because I was one of the stars of the tour and there was bound to be some disappointment over my injury. I was supposed to say a few words, tell everyone what happened, and then we could get on with the end of show. So what did I do? Basically I incited a riot, first by using a shovel to decapitate a flag-waving robot that was part of the show; then by urging fans to "storm the stadium and attack!"

A brilliant idea: give several thousand drunken Aussie freestyle motocross fans an excuse to unleash mayhem, and they're probably going to do it. The next thing I knew, fans were streaming out of the stands and onto the field, and the riot police were on their way.

I got out of there as quickly as I could. Before I left the stadium, though, I had ol' Felix the Cat hit me up with a shot of morphine. Then Deegan and I found a couple of chicks in the crowd and had them give us a ride back to the hotel. The last thing I remember about that night was pulling into a gas station, and hearing one of the girls asking Brian, "What's wrong with your friend? Is he okay?"

I was on the edge of unconsciousness, the opiates flowing through my body, warm and soothing, killing the pain in my foot and elsewhere.

"Don't worry about him," Brian said. "He's just a little tired."

The next day I woke to a firestorm. Everyone was pissed at me: the promoters, the other riders, Jon and Dana. And who could blame them? If I were them, I would have kicked in the door to my hotel room and smashed the living shit out of me for being such an irresponsible punk with no regard for anyone else. It was disgusting the way that I was behaving. I was making the sport look bad, and I was making my friends and employers look bad. They should have kicked my ass.

Instead, they nearly gave me a get-out-of-jail-free card; they were going to let everything slide. But then the promoters decided that I should pay for at least some of the damage. They also wanted me off the tour. My response was that of a typical drug addict, unwilling to take responsibility for anything. I was a walking, talking rationalization.

Why are you guys yelling at me when this is really what you want? You expect this out of me. Don't act surprised now.

I'd managed to collect a substantial portion of my fee up front (again, this was duplicitous, since I had no intention of jumping), so I decided to leave immediately. And I tried to convince Deegan to join me.

"Brian, check this out. I am out of here. I got my money and I'm gonna bounce. You with me?"

He wasn't interested, so I booked a flight to Melbourne, where I had some connections.

I arrived with about fifteen grand—cash—in my pocket, and no plans other than to find enough narcotics to get me through the next few days. The sickness had already set in by the time the plane touched down, so I didn't waste a minute before calling my contact. This guy was not a drug dealer; he owned a brothel. But I knew from experience that if you were new in town, and you really needed drugs, there was no more efficient conduit than the local prostitutes. So I feigned interest in getting laid.

"Come on down," he said. "We'll get you all set up. You don't even have to pay. Just tip the girls well."

They paraded past in various degrees of undress. I barely noticed whether they were attractive or not, since my focus was not on their breasts or backsides, but rather on their forearms and wrists, maybe the backs of their knees—bumps of hardened skin, the telltale signs of a fellow junkie. Finally this cute girl named Miley walked up to me. She seemed to meet the criteria.

"Hey sweetheart, you want a room?"

"Look, I'll be straight up with you. I'm not here for that. I need to score some dope."

She frowned.

"Shhhh! Don't talk like that around here, okay?"

"Sorry."

"All right," she said. "Get a room and I'll be right in."

The party began shortly thereafter, and lasted for the better part of a month. Miley turned out to be some sort of Melbourne heroin queen who worked with the Asian mafia. But what a contradictory life she led! Miley invited me home that evening after we both got loaded. (I kept waking her up because she was so smacked out.) When the cab pulled up in front of her address, it was not the shitty ghetto flat I expected, but rather a neat little house. Inside were Mom and Dad, and a dining room table set for dinner.

Holy crap! This chick's got a normal family.

"Hey, Mom," Miley said. "This is Larry. He's gonna stay with us for a while."

Mom extended her hand warmly and smiled, like this wasn't even an unusual occurrence.

"Nice to meet you, Larry. We'll be having dinner shortly."

So we all sat down together, me and Miley and her mom and dad. But Miley kept nodding off, so I had to carry the conversation alone.

"How do you know our daughter, Larry?"

"Oh, I met her through a friend."

"And what do you do for a living?"

"I ride motorcycles," I told them, and then I asked if they had ever heard of the Crusty Demons Tour. They said that they had. "Well, I'm part of that," I said, which of course was no longer true, but sounded pretty good.

It was all intensely weird, hanging out at the home of this chick I had just met, eating dinner with her perfectly pleasant and normal parents while she was passed out at the table, trying to figure out how to explain to Mom and Dad how I fucking met her, without telling the truth.

Actually, we met at brothel and did a bunch of heroin together, and she's bringing me back because I just robbed my promoters and I have nowhere to go and I am trying not to be dope sick. Could you pass the potatoes, please?

After dinner, I roused Miley and we went into her room, which was painted pink and decorated like a normal teenage girl's room, right down to the Hello

Kitty paraphernalia. On a nightstand next to the bed, however, was paraphernalia of a different sort: crack pipes and sterile needles, and all kinds of other junkie shit.

Whoa . . . man. This is too bizarre.

But it wasn't. Not for this particular family, which apparently had made peace with their daughter's chosen lifestyle. I'm a father now, so I sort of get it. You do what you can to keep your kid safe and alive, even if it means tolerating her drug use and prostitution. Guess they figured she was less likely to die if she was under their roof. Miley would get up in the morning (or early afternoon) and her mom would drive her to the whorehouse. Talk about enabling! It was one of the strangest things I have ever seen, and that's saying something. It was even kind of sobering for me. I didn't want to get too close to Miley because she was so whacked out, and dealing intimately with so many bad and dangerous people. My drug use actually diminished a bit while I was in Melbourne. I'd be like, "Come on, Miley, I'll fight the kick a little if you fight it, too."

I hated doing drugs in their house when they were feeding me and being so nice to me. I felt like I was the bad influence, when in reality, Miley had sunk to a level of depravity far below anything I'd experienced. She'd meet up with her Asian connections and come back with bricks of heroin. Then we'd cut them up together in her bedroom and shoot up. Our relationship was strictly platonic. We shared a bedroom, even a bed. But we never had sex. Not once. We were friends . . . drug buddies. Our entire relationship revolved around getting loaded.

It's so hard to explain how you get to that point, how drugs can take over your life. I went from being a total anti-drug guy—a guy who hated needles and always wanted to be in control—to someone who spent a month living with a heroin-trafficking prostitute. I was the guy who used to show up at parties and scoff at the junky scumbag passed out in the corner. Then I became the junky scumbag, showing up loaded at events, with a giant, dripping syringe painted on the side of my bike, shooting up in front of people. And I was proud of my transformation. Which just goes to show, once you are consumed by drugs, anything can happen.

CHAPTER 12

One day in the fall of 2001, Brian Deegan stopped by my place all worked up over an open audition for a movie that supposedly would have some connection to the freestyle motocross world. Not a little movie, he explained. A big Hollywood production. And they needed real riders to handle some of the stunt work.

"Cool, have fun," I said.

"No, man. You gotta come with me. I don't want to go alone."

"Dude, I'm not going to audition for some movie. I have no interest in that."

The conversation went on in that manner for the better part of ten minutes. Brian could be a persuasive and manipulative little fuck when he wanted something, and eventually he wore me down.

"I already put your bike in the back of my truck," he said. "Let's just go. Please?"

"Oh, all right."

So we hopped in the truck and drove down to Perris Raceway. I could not possibly have been less interested in this adventure. But Brian was still my friend and business partner, so I wanted to support him. Metal Mulisha by this time had really started to take off; we were moving a fair amount of product, although any money that came in was quickly funneled right back into the business, to help it grow. Or so I was told anyway—Brian handled most of the financial details; I trusted him (which would turn out to be a mistake). Unlike me, Brian had continued to stay active in the competitive freestyle world, so his name and face had become synonymous with the Metal Mulisha. He was fairly smooth, too. Really knew how to play the game with distributors and sponsors, as well as the media. Sure, he had a drug problem, too, but it wasn't nearly as debilitating as mine had become. Brian understood the value of promotion, especially self-promotion, and he naturally viewed participation in a big-budget movie as an ideal opportunity for publicity. And, of course, he wanted to stroke his own ego. For most people, it would be a trip to appear in a movie; Brian was no different in that regard. Me? I didn't give a shit.

I didn't say much on the forty-minute ride to Perris Raceway. I was disinterested and grumpy, in part because I was on little more than a maintenance dose of opiates, which left me feeling relatively clear-headed, but also a bit queasy. Following the debacle in Australia, there had been an intervention, led by my buddy Phil, who was himself still heavily into all kinds of drugs, but apparently of the opinion that my situation was significantly worse. He was probably right. So Phil had rolled up one day in his corvette and strong-armed me into going to rehab. It was a fairly brief stay—really just a way to safely detox—and certainly did nothing to alter my perception about drugs. I was hardly committed to making any great changes in my life. But I did want to scale back a bit, and this first stint in rehab (there would be others) helped me do that. So on this particular day, as I rumbled grumpily along in Deegan's truck, I would have been classified as more of a drug user than a drug addict.

It might sound like a subtle distinction, unless you've been in both camps.

At the time I was not so strung out on drugs that I couldn't ride. I mean, I was in no shape to attempt anything too dangerous or innovative, but I could ride a little bit. It wasn't like Australia, where I'd been virtually incapacitated. So I figured I'd tag along with Brian and do whatever he asked, just to keep him happy, and then get the hell out of there.

Although Perris Raceway had been a big part of my adolescence, I hadn't been there in a while. On this day it had been transformed into a freestyle park, with a bunch of jumps and the whole freestyle community in attendance. Some of these guys were my friends, some I detested. All of them seemed nervous and excited. Honestly, I think I was the only person there who truly did not give a shit. And maybe there's a lesson there.

The stunt coordinator on the project (and that's all it was to me—a project; I had no idea what the film was called, or who would be appearing in it) eventually gathered everyone together. I was a little late to the meeting, and when I arrived I introduced myself by asking, "Which one of these assholes are you going to choose?"

He smiled, said he hadn't made up his mind yet, and then asked my name.

"Larry Linkogle."

"Hi, Larry. I'm Lance Gilbert. You going to ride today or are you just here to bust everyone's balls?"

I looked around. Sober, I was as good a rider as any of these guys; better than most.

"Sure, why not? Long as I'm here, right?"

Lance nodded. "Good luck."

There were no detailed instructions. Basically they just wanted us to ride around for a while, hit some jumps, do some tricks, give them an opportunity to watch and evaluate. We didn't know how many riders they needed, or what the job would entail. We were simply told to ride. The blanks would be filled in later.

So I rode with some of my friends, didn't attempt anything too strenuous, and certainly didn't feel like I was involved in any sort of "audition." I was just trying to have some fun. Everyone else seemed deadly serious, like they were involved in some life-changing contest. After a while someone on the crew asked me to stop, then stuck a camera and microphone in my face, and asked me to recite a couple lines. I fucked that up, laughed it off, and went back to riding. Brian actually kept his distance. After begging me to join him, I think he was probably a little bit embarrassed at the way I was acting, and so he tried to pretend like he barely knew me—guilt by association, I guess.

The whole thing lasted only a couple hours and soon we were back on the road, heading home to Temecula with our bikes in the back of Brian's truck.

"How do you think I did?" he asked, his voice betraying his anxiety.

"I don't know, Brian. I wasn't watching."

"Yeah, I think that guy liked me. I've got a good shot, right?

"No doubt, dude."

We got home, unloaded the bikes, and I put the whole thing out of my mind. It wasn't until the next day, when the phone rang, that I discovered just how odd a world Hollywood can be.

"Is this Larry?"

"Yes, it is."

"Hi, Larry. Lance Gilbert here."

"Oh, hey, Lance. How's it going? You find your guy?

"As a matter of fact, yeah, I think so."

As usual, I was a little slow on the uptake. "Cool. I'm sure he's going to be stoked."

"Yeah, I hope so. See, we kind of think you fit the image."

I tried to let that sink in. "What image?"

Lance went on to explain that they needed a stunt rider to stand in for the film's star, and that of all the people who had auditioned, I was the best fit.

"The main character is a taller guy, kind of thick," he said. He's a muscular guy, a bit stocky. And you know, out of everyone there, you were the only one with a big frame.

This was true. A lot of riders are shorter, with a lower center of gravity.

Many of them are muscular but wiry. At this time I was about six foot two, 220 pounds.

"Plus you're a good rider," Lance added. Then he paused. "Look, Larry, I'll be honest with you. A big part of the reason people get picked for parts isn't so much because of their talent; it's the way they look, and whether or not the stunt coordinator or the director likes them. We all want someone who's easy to get along with."

How about that? Irreverence and apathy had gotten me the job. Sometimes life is weird.

———————

As soon as I got off the phone I ran down the street to Brian's house (we lived on the same block). I didn't want to rub anything in his face; money was an issue for me and the income that would be generated by this job would come in handy. And anyway, if the situation had been reversed and Brian had gotten the call, I would have been happy for him. To put it mildly, though, Brian was not amused.

"Guess what?" I said.

"What?"

"They fucking called me!"

"Who?"

"Lance—the guy from the movie. I got the part! Can you believe it?! After all the shit I was talking?"

"Dude . . . come on."

And then Brian went off, walking around the house, shaking his head, muttering under his breath.

"This is ridiculous. You wouldn't even have known about this if it weren't for me."

He had a point. The truth is, I wouldn't have gotten the offer if it weren't for Brian. And when I saw just how badly he was hurt by all of this, I wanted to help him. He was my friend, after all, and it obviously meant a lot more to him than it did to me.

"Okay, Brian. I'll see if I can get you included."

At my next meeting with Lance Gilbert, I asked if there might be room in the budget for a backup, someone who could serve as my backup in the event of an injury, and help me out with setup and other details. Lance agreed that this was a good idea, but disagreed with Brian as the choice. By this time, I had learned the star of the movie was Vin Diesel, and the simple fact was this: physically, there was no way for Brian to work as a stand-in for Vin Diesel. The actor was six feet tall and weighed more than two hundred pounds. Brian was about five foot nine, 175 pounds.

"He just doesn't fit," Lance said. "Pick someone else."

So I chose Twitch (who was roughly six feet tall), which predictably enraged Brian.

"Don't worry, man," I told him. "We'll squeeze you in somewhere. I promise."

It all got very complicated. The producers wanted to rent a mobile landing ramp that Brian and I had recently purchased through the company, and Brian tried to charge them an exorbitant fee for its use. Eventually they came to some sort of a compromise that included Brian getting a part as an extra in a party scene, along with a speaking line (although it ended up on the cutting room floor). And I hooked up a bunch of my friends with jobs as extras; they also helped with set up, so they got to hang around on set for a few days and soak up the movie-star atmosphere, and make a few bucks in the process.

The name of the film was *Triple X*, and it featured Vin Diesel as a character named Xander Cage, "an extreme sports athlete recruited by the government on a special mission." My job was to fill in for Diesel when the script called for the character to ride his motorcycle in a series of dangerous stunts. I was simply a hired gun, but I was given significant input when it came to designing equipment for the stunts and ensuring that they were properly and safely executed. Truthfully, though, none of it seemed particularly difficult or risky. These were ordinary jumps and tricks executed in a controlled, non-competitive environment; no big deal at all, not even for a guy who had spent only minimal time on his bike in the previous year.

In the first week of December 2001, I showed up on the set, which was located in Ventura County, not far from the Magic Mountain amusement park. I was able to get out and test the ramps and get a feel for the first stunt in advance of filming. I spent hours in the make-up chair having molds taken so that the artists could design a prosthetic Vin Diesel mask for me to wear. We ran into a little snag when they decided to shave my head so that I'd look more like Vin (who usually runs bald). Suddenly they got a good look at the demon tattoo, which I had neglected to mention on the job application.

"Are you kidding me?" one of the makeup artists said. "What the hell are we supposed to do with this?"

It really wasn't that big of a deal—I think they were just a little surprised. A splash of makeup and we were good to go. There were several scenes to film, a bunch of different tricks, all relatively uncomplicated and well within my comfort zone, presuming everything went as it was supposed to go. I remember feeling confident and clear-headed during that whole experience, although, as I said, I wasn't completely clean. I was taking just enough painkillers to avoid getting dope sick, which was, at times, a bit of a high-wire act. At one point, I approached Brian Manley on the set to see if he could hook me up with some Vicodin. Brian had suffered a broken back a couple years earlier when he took a fall in Phoenix; the accident had left him with partial paralysis and obviously ended his riding career. He usually got around on crutches. But he was still a smart guy who knew how to build ramps and design courses. And he was my buddy, so I brought him in to help on the movie. Like anyone with that severe an injury, Brian also had legitimate access to painkillers, so I tried to hit him up.

But Brian knew me well enough by then.

"No fuckin' way, dude. I'm not gonna help you get loaded. Not here."

When it came time to film the first trick, I was surprised to learn that they did not want me to wear a helmet. That's why they'd made such a fuss about the makeup and the tattoo—Vin's character in the movie was supposed to ride without a helmet, so I'd have to perform in the same way, while serving as his stunt double. Given my generally self-destructive nature, and the various ways in which I'd tried to do damage to my body, you might think this wouldn't have bothered me in the least. But it did. Big time.

"No one ever said anything about going without a helmet," I said to Lance Gilbert. "I am not cool with that."

Lance is a great guy, totally cool about working with all kinds of people. He's a pro, and I know he understood my trepidation. Still, if the director needed a shot without a helmet, that's the way we were going to do it. I sought a compromise.

"How about we just do this," I said. "Let me at least wear my helmet for the rehearsals, you know? And roll the tape while we're doing it. For the main deal, I'll do it with no helmet. Just one take. But let's at least try to even out the risk, you know?"

Lance nodded. "No, you're right. That's completely fair."

So Lance chatted with the director, Rob Cohen, and he agreed with that plan. It was prudent, sensible, and would still give him the naked image he'd need when we went hot. My job was to hit the stunt perfectly; everything else was out of my control.

On the first stunt, my character was supposed to jump over a flatbed truck containing a load of cocaine while getting chased and shot at by a helicopter. For dramatic impact the truck would get hit by gunfire and explode while I soared over it. Then I'd land and ride off. That was the plan anyway. I'd already tested the ramps earlier in the day and felt comfortable with the whole setup.

The rehearsal process was methodical and professional. I hit the jump alone while the cameras rolled, so that they could get the proper angles and adjust to my timing. Then they brought in the helicopter. The idea was that the pilot would fly alongside me while I hit the jump and figure out the proper speed for the shot. We did that a couple times, everyone seemed comfortable, and the director called for another pass, this one with the helicopter trailing me, close behind, just as it would appear in the movie. In effect this was the final rehearsal. Then we'd go hot.

That's the way I understood it anyway. Later there would be some confusion and dispute about exactly what was expected on this run. A few people on the set claimed that I was actually supposed to run up to the jump and wait, allowing the helicopter to pass overhead without any interference. Whether someone on the stunt team misinterpreted the instructions, I don't know. What I do know is what they said: "The pilot will track you, chase you, and then you're going to jump. Just like in the movie. We'll do that once, and then we're going hot."

It all made sense to me.

So I hit the throttle, leaned into the handlebars, and rolled toward the ramp. I hit it perfectly, thought everything was fine. I was soaring, climbing, waiting to stall out for the landing . . . when suddenly, out of the corner of my eye, I could see the front edge of the helicopter, just overhead and way too close.

Oh, fuck . . .

I tried to crouch low, pulling my head down and into the handlebars. I had crashed enough times to know the feeling of impending disaster. Time really does stand still. You can see the accident coming, and your brain focuses with white-hot intensity on trying to figure out an exit strategy. But there were few options. When a helicopter hits a motorcycle, the motorcycle loses. All I could hope to do was minimize the contact by making myself as small as possible.

Most freestyle crashes are fairly quiet—the sound of metal against dirt. This one was different, the sound of metal against metal, a terrible, high-pitch screeching sound as my head hit the bottom of the chopper. And then there was another sound, like something scraping, as I hit the guard rails.

I was instantly dazed to the point of disorientation, like when you get hit in the head during a fight. There was tremendous pressure in my ears and sinuses, and the feeling of being underwater. Then everything went dark . . . and then light again.

It's called a "flash knockout," a brief loss of consciousness, and while it's not pleasant, it's not as bad as being knocked out cold, especially if you're thirty feet in the air on the seat of a motorcycle. I remember snapping back to life and feeling a sudden sense of tranquility, like everything would be okay. The slow motion continued as I ran through a mental checklist: find the landing area, ease upon the grip on the handlebars, get up off the seat . . . all basic stuff. There was just one problem: I couldn't find the landing area. The impact had pushed me off line and catapulted me forward, so instead of easing into a nicely positioned landing ramp, I was going to hit the flats.

Shit! This is going to be bad . . .

I remember hitting the ground and bouncing hard. Then I lost consciousness again. When I woke, I was on the ground, next to my bike, and people were standing over me, asking if I was all right. My helmet was destroyed. As dizzy and disoriented as I was, I immediately thought about what would have happened if I had gone bare-headed as originally planned. I'd have been killed, for sure. Instead I'd merely been concussed, although I didn't realize at the time just how serious an injury it was. After any crash the first thing you do is try to remain calm and do a self-assessment of what might be wrong.

Okay, I can move my arms. That's good. My legs are working. That's good, too. No blood, so that's a relief. Shoulder is sore, but not too bad . . .

You don't want to be a tough guy and jump to your feet, because if you do have a broken bone or torn ligaments, you're likely to make the problem even worse. Plus it hurts like hell. So I just sat there for a while. I didn't know exactly what had happened, but I did know that I'd collided with a helicopter, so the possibility existed that I'd been seriously hurt. I waited for the warm, sickening feeling that comes with a gaping wound. But it didn't happen.

The accident must have looked absolutely terrifying, because everyone froze in its aftermath. A minute or more passed before anyone came to my side. The first person I saw was Brian Manley. He had tears in his eyes.

"Are you okay, man?"

"Yeah . . . I think so."

Lance Gilbert and Rob Cohen were both great about making sure I was not seriously injured, trying to provide comfort and asking if I needed anything. Today, of course, an incident such as this would likely be handled much differently. If a stunt rider were to get hit by a helicopter, he'd immediately be brought to a hospital for tests and observation, regardless of his appearance. We simply shut down filming for the night and I went back to my hotel room. I later found out from several sources that the accident could have been so much worse. At some point I'd been clipped by a metal guard that shields the rear rotor. Not all helicopters have this guard; without it, I'd have been decapitated, and the pilot might have lost control of the chopper and crashed into the set, perhaps killing dozens of film crew workers.

All things considered, we'd been lucky.

A nurse on the set gave me a couple Vicodin before I left the set (which I really did need, both for the pain in my shoulders and knee after the crash, and because I had basically run out of opiates). She asked once more if I wanted to go to the hospital. I said I'd be fine and went back to the hotel to sleep.

And then things got really weird.

On the thirty-minute drive back to the hotel (yes, I did drive myself, which is kind of nuts when you think about it), my vision began to blur. I started seeing double. At the same time, I came to an awareness of what had just transpired. I thought about the way everyone had reacted on the set, and how scared and concerned they'd been, and finally I realized just how close I'd come to dying. And then, right there in the car, I began to cry. I can't explain it. I suppose it had something to do with coming to terms with my own mortality, but I also think it was related to the fact that my brain had been sloshed around in my skull.

I felt helpless. I had no control over my emotions. And I remember thinking, *Dude, why are you being such a little bitch? Stop fucking crying!*

But I couldn't. When I got back to my room I called my mom and told her all about the accident. She was scared but relieved that I was apparently all right. I told her that I loved her and my dad, which was not something I'd ever done before. Not in years anyway.

Then I tried to lie down and close my eyes, but the bed kept spinning, like I was drunk or something. I had to put one foot on the floor to make it stop. Eventually the walls stopped moving and I fell asleep.

━━━━━━━

I woke to a darkened room, the blinds pulled tight, and the air stale and sour. I looked at the clock: 7:30. As I threw back the covers and started to move, I felt a coldness on my legs. The sheets and mattress were soaked, and my thighs were chafed and red.

Holy shit—I wet the bed.

If this has never happened to you, consider yourself lucky. And trust me: there's nothing like pissing yourself to make you realize that something has gone very wrong. I got out of bed and tried to walk to the bathroom, but the entire room seemed to be titled at a forty-five-degree angle. I kept bumping into the walls and furniture. This would go on for weeks. I existed in a world tilted on its axis, everything slightly out of place. I kept banging into walls and furniture and other people. Classic signs of a concussion, at the very least, and maybe something much more sinister. But I basically ignored the symptoms and tried to get on with work and life.

After going to the bathroom and cleaning myself up, I walked back into the room and threw open the blinds. To my dismay and surprise, it was dark outside. We had been shooting at night and so I hadn't gotten back to my room until after midnight. I had presumed that the wetness and headache had woken me after only a few hours of sleep. Uh-uh. It was 7:30 at night! I'd been asleep for roughly eighteen hours. Again, not a good sign.

I grabbed my cell phone: there were nearly fifty missed calls. I was already late to the set, so I taped up my swollen knee, got dressed, and hopped in the car. I drove straight to the set, all the while trying not to hit any of the cars that came at me sideways on the highway. I knew that my brain was on vacation, but I went to work anyway, hiding my symptoms and discomfort. When I arrived on the set, everyone treated me with care and concern. Lance Gilbert gave me an opportunity to back out, but I said I was fine. When Rob Cohen stopped by, I feigned anger and gave him a hard look.

"Hope you guys got some good lawyers, because I'm going to sue your asses."

Rob stared at me blankly. I could tell he was really nervous, so I didn't leave him hanging.

"Nah, I'm just fucking with you, dude. I wouldn't sue you guys. Accidents happen."

He smiled, let out a nervous little laugh. "Don't screw around like that, Larry. We're all really worried about you."

"Hey, I'm good. Don't worry. Let's get to work."

I obviously shouldn't have been joking like that about something so serious, but I was trying to relieve some of the tension. Lance and Rob both asked if I wanted to do a couple more trial runs, before shooting the stunt, but I declined.

"I'm ready to go hot. Let's just do it."

The truth is, I felt like crap, and I figured the less time I spent on the bike, the better. I wanted to hit my jumps and get the hell out of there as quickly as possible. Even with a headache and blurred vision, I figured I could spank it out, no problem, save my reputation and get paid, and get everyone off the hook.

"Just keep that fucking chopper away from me, okay?" I said it with a smile, but I wasn't kidding. In reality, though, I knew the chances of getting hit again were practically non-existent. Extraordinary caution would be exercised by everyone involved. So I hit the makeup chair, put on my Vin Diesel mask and wardrobe, and got ready to jump the exploding cocaine truck all over again. No helmet this time. I just rode out and did it live, nailed the first take perfectly. I flew through the blast and the pyro with the helicopter giving chase and landed smoothly. I could hear the crew applauding and cheering as I cruised away.

Fuck, yeah!

The feeling of accomplishment was significant, especially under the circumstances. I got to review the footage with Lance and Rob, and see how the stunt came together perfectly. There was no doubt in my mind that it was going to work beautifully in the movie. And I was part of it. Despite nearly getting killed the previous day, I'd come through for these guys. I think they appreciated that. I felt good about myself, despite feeling like shit. I mean, when I got off the bike and everyone started patting me on the back, freaking out because the shot looked so fucking cool, I could feel myself listing to the side again.

Everything was sideways. I had lost my depth perception, too. An object ten feet in the distance appeared to be twenty feet away. Or five feet away. Didn't matter. The point is, I was in no shape to ride. One more stunt was on the schedule for that night, a big jump over a barn. I really wanted to do this stunt; it was one of the biggest scenes in the movie. But I was getting worse by the second. I tried timing the jump a few times in practice but bailed every time. There was just no way to get it down with my vision the way it was. Finally I approached one of the assistant producers and told him I wasn't feeling well. I glossed over the details because I was worried they might insist I go to the hospital and I'd be off the movie for the rest of the shoot. So I just said I was a little woozy and tired. Given what had happened the previous night, and the fact that I had already nailed the first stunt, everyone was more than accommodating.

"Why don't you just give this one to Twitch, and I'll take the day off, okay?"

"Sure, Link. No problem."

Twitch absolutely killed the jump. I was happy for him, but naturally a little disappointed for myself. And it went on that way for the better part of a week, with the two of us trading off on stunts, and me trying desperately not to let anyone know the extent of my disability. (Incidentally, after the second day, someone made a decision that we would wear helmets on all of the jumps.) Near the end of the shoot I finally confessed to Lance about the headaches and dizziness, and he insisted that I go to the hospital. The docs looked me over, took some X-rays, declared my skull to be free of fractures, said there was no indication of bleeding, and sent me on my way with some pain pills.

They were wrong, of course. There was, as it turned out, significant damage. It would be years before I'd get the proper diagnosis. In the meantime, I would wobble and stagger through life, not merely a drug addict, but a drug addict with a traumatic brain injury.

CHAPTER 13

Mykella and I had first met in the fall of 2001, when the Survivor Tour passed through Las Vegas. The Survivor Tour was designed to cash in on the reality television craze that was first beginning to sweep the nation (or at least the airwaves). Twenty of the top freeriders and freestylists in the motocross game (divided into teams of four) would spend roughly two weeks on the road, stopping in ten different cities, assembling highlight reels of tricks and jumps at each site, and then putting those videos out for the world to see. Fans would vote for the favorites and eventually the field would be winnowed and someone would be declared the Survivor champion.

That someone was me.

But that's not the point. The point is that I met the woman who would become my second wife and the mother of my son while on the Survivor Tour. "Kella" lived in Huntington Beach but was working as an exotic dancer in Vegas at the time. What can I tell you—it wasn't exactly a fairytale romance. The Survivor Tour was on its way to Utah. We had some time to kill, and so we naturally ended up where guys end up in Vegas: at a strip joint.

Kella was just one of the girls in the mix that night, although super smokin' hot and a formidable partier. This was between Australia and the *Triple X* incident, so I wasn't completely consumed by drugs. I guess you'd say I was in a state of relatively quiet maintenance, which is why I was able to ride well enough to win the Survivor Tour. But I wasn't sober, that's for sure. The night we went out in Vegas, I did some Norcos and cocaine, spent a lot of time hanging out with Kella, and just sort of got hooked on her, you know. Not in a serious way, but in a sexual, partying kind of way. She was a fun chick, blond and angular, with a fair amount of ink, but didn't look too hard yet, the way some strippers do.

At some point during the night a bunch of the guys on the Survivor Tour ended up at Carey Hart's house. Carey was another rider and he lived in Vegas, so a bunch of us were crashing at his place before hitting the road the next day. I remember doing a few lines of coke with the boys and then for some reason getting this crazy idea to take Kella with me.

"Yo, Carey," I said. "Check this out. I'm gonna go get that chick and bring her back here."

"What chick?"

"The stripper—Kella."

Carey laughed and put up his hands. "No, no, no. Don't be fucking stupid, man."

"I'm serious, dude. And I might even bring her out on the road."

Everyone started howling, calling me all kinds of names, telling me I was out of my fucking mind. I don't even know if I was serious about it at first, but their reaction for some reason strengthened my resolve.

"No joke. I'm going to call her."

And so I did.

I told her we'd be meeting up at Carey's place at noon the next day, and she was welcome to join us. She asked if she could bring a friend along.

"Sure, why not? I'll go to bat for both of you."

I don't really know whether I expected them to show up or not, but sure as shit, around noon, Kella and her friend rolled up with their little stripper suitcases, ready to join the Survivor Tour.

"Come on," I said. "You can both share the top bunk with me."

Hungover and not particularly concerned with how the addition of two strippers might impact anyone else on the tour, I welcomed them both aboard our bus, which was more like a traveling hotel. Before we all had a chance to settle in, however, I was approached by Dana Nicholson and Jon Freeman. They pulled me aside and quietly but firmly let me know that Kella and her friend were not welcome.

"Larry," they said. "You've gotta be kidding. Those two chicks are not coming on the bus."

"Why not?" I said, feigning ignorance. "They're with me."

"Yeah, that doesn't matter. We can't have strippers on the tour bus."

I wasn't about to fight for them. I mean, it wasn't really that important to me. As usual, I was in a questionable mental state and did not comprehend the implications of my actions, or simply didn't care. Jon and Dana had families— wives and children. Obviously they didn't want strippers on the bus, especially when the entire trip was being captured on video and much of it was being broadcast on live television. Sure, we were freeriders and partiers by definition, but I can imagine that for the married guys on the crew, the idea of having their wives watching the show back home, and seeing strippers roll on up to the tour bus, might cause some problems.

So I explained the situation to Kella, escorted her off the bus, and left her in Vegas. To be perfectly honest, I never expected to see her again. It wasn't like I'd fallen in love or anything; I just wanted someone cute to hang with on the road. And whatever else Kella might have been, she was cute as hell.

Months passed. Kella became a distant memory, so much so that when a couple of my friends told me that they had run into some chick from Huntington Beach who knew me, I didn't even know who they were talking about.

"Yeah, this girl loves you, man. Said you met her in Vegas and promised to take her on the road with you."

I had to think long and hard. Then I remembered.

"Oh, yeah . . . the stripper."

"Hot chick. She wants your phone number."

At first I said yes. Then I said no. Then I said yes again. For some reason, I was apprehensive about revisiting that territory. Anyway, one day I got a phone call from Kella. At the time, I was in Huntington Beach, hanging out with a mixed martial artist who at one time had been a legitimate contender. Let's just call him Stan the Man. He was one of those guys who preferred dying in the ring to surrendering or quitting. Stan was a mentor to Phil Ensminger, and very nearly as wild and violent. The two of them used to get cocaine from this dude they called "the short, fat, laughing man." Because . . . well, the guy was short and fat and used to laugh a lot. The short, fat, laughing man would make deliveries in something they called "the dirty sock"—basically a chunk of cocaine in a bag. Stan would use his knife to slice off a sliver of coke, like he was shaving a wedge of cheese.

Peru had spoiled me when it came coke, but if it was available—and it was always available when you were with Stan and Phil—I'd do some. I mean, I'd do almost anything—I was a drug addict. So we were at Stan's place, getting fucked up, when Kella called.

"You should come on over," she said. "Bring your friends. We'll party."

She had a nice townhouse in Huntington Beach and basically I just went up there one night and didn't leave for a few weeks. We partied, went to bed, and I woke up the next morning to the sight of Kella cooking breakfast for me. I was hooked. She was a beautiful girl, didn't care whether I did drugs or not, and seemed to have her shit together. As it turned out, this was not at all the case. Kella was crazy as all fuck. She was basically like an extra dude thrown into the mix, except she was incredibly hot. And she was such an enabler that she'd even go to Dr. Kevorkian with me so that we could get double prescriptions.

I didn't know at the time that she was also fighting a felony DUI hit-and-run. Nor did I realize that she was a stripper mom. That little nugget of information was revealed when I got tired of Huntington Beach and moved back to Temecula, with Kella in tow.

"I need to get my kids' stuff out of storage," she said.

That should have been a red flag. But it wasn't. Not even the use of the plural—*kids*, as in more than one—dissuaded me. Although only in her mid-twenties, Kella had two children. Both lived with their fathers—one in Washington State, the other in Orange, California. (The girl in California was five years old when I met Kella, and eventually spent a lot of time living with us; I was her dad for a while, although not a very good one.)

My parents were not thrilled about my relationship with Kella; nor were my friends.

"What are you fucking doing, man? This chick is no good for you. You need to get her on the road."

"Yeah? Well fuck you guys! I'm keeping her around."

And so I did. It was about as unhealthy and dysfunctional a relationship as you could ever expect to find. In the first six months we bounced back and forth from Temecula to Huntington Beach as Kella served a couple months in jail for her felony DUI. I did a stint in rehab and then got mangled on the set of *Triple X*. Then I fell back into a pattern of deepening drug use, and was riding only sporadically.

Through Phil I picked up work—always off the books—doing construction, but just enough to keep me in drugs. Metal Mulisha, by this time, had begun generating revenue, but I never saw much of it. My partnership (and friendship) with Brian Deegan deteriorated rapidly, to the point that eventually I was locked out of my own business. To some extent, I take the blame for this. I was more concerned with chasing the next high and feeding my drug habit than I was with riding or building a company. I wasn't paying attention and thus failed to notice that my best friend and partner had begun working toward a business model that would not include me, despite the fact that I had created the business in the first place. I acknowledge that I was a handful in those days. Brian wasn't exactly an angel either, but he could be charming and funny, and generally presented to the corporate world a more reliable and marketable image. He was also a skilled politician—willing and able to talk about himself in big terms, while deflecting any criticism about the company toward me, an easy solution since I was an acknowledged fuck-up. This resulted in a huge rift within the Metal Mulisha: Brian's friends and advocates on one side, my friends and advocates on the other side.

Since Brian had the corporate backing and the money, you can imagine which side had more followers.

It fell apart slowly . . . and then all at once.

By that I mean it seemed to me that the dissolution of our partnership and friendship came out of the blue, but that's only because I was sleepwalking through life.

There was a phone call one afternoon in 2002. Brian invited me to a meeting. Said he wanted to discuss a bunch of new business opportunities for the Mulisha. There would be lawyers and managers and other hotshots from the entertainment industry. Included in this group was Bob Dylan's son, Jesse Dylan, who was building a name for himself as a producer, director, and overall media heavyweight. It turned out that Brian had already taken numerous meetings with Jesse and others, and that they were interested in helping to develop the Metal Mulisha brand. But it was also about developing the career of Brian Deegan. There was talk of book deals and movies, reality television shows, all featuring Brian in service of the Mulisha brand. He would be out front; I would be in the background.

Way in the background.

Which was okay. I wasn't seeking fame or fortune; I wasn't into self-aggrandizement. To a fault, I didn't give a shit about my own reputation or success. And I trusted Brian to do what was best for the company and everyone who worked and rode for the Mulisha. Hell, he was my best buddy; he wouldn't fuck me over.

Right?

No one was all that interested in talking with me. Jesse Dylan seemed to have no respect for me whatsoever. I mean, he respected me in a thug way—like, he was nervous that I might lose control and hurt him—but as far as respect in a business sense? Uh-uh. Not in the least. He spoke to me in a condescending manner, like he presumed that I had no intelligence.

I realize now, looking back on it, that there was something else at work; I think everyone at the meeting understood that I was a dead man walking; I was on my way out the door of the company and didn't even know it.

This guy is a fucking idiot. We can do whatever we want to him and he'll never catch on to it.

At the same time they were thoroughly impressed by Brian, who worked the room smoothly, shaking hands, making small talk, perpetuating the image of a man in control. It probably seemed as though he had created and built the Metal Mulisha, while I was just tagging along. He was the great white shark; I was the little sucker fish attached to his back, getting a free ride.

While I sensed this attitude, I didn't really give it much thought. I figured my friendship with Brian was solid and that if things progressed with the company, that would be good for everyone. I didn't really care that I was perceived as lesser partner. I let Brian work the room, shake as many hands as he wanted to shake, while I kept a low profile.

Not long after that, I got another call from Brian. He was having a party at his place and wanted me to come over. So I did. Soon as I arrived, someone offered me a few shots of Jäger. I happily obliged, got a little fucked up (and of course I was already somewhat fucked up to begin with), and we hung out for the night. Finally, around two o'clock in the morning, I got up to leave.

"Man, I'm calling it a night," I said to Brian. "I'm pretty torqued. Think I'll just walk home." (We still lived in the same neighborhood.)

"Yeah, that's cool. Before you go, can do something for me?"

"Sure, dude. Anything."

He pulled out a sheath of papers. "I need you to sign this."

"What is it?"

He said it was no big deal, just a new contract for the LLC, one that would protect us better if we ever get sued.

"Who would sue us?"

Brian laughed. "Ah, you never know dude."

Brian was my closest friend. Hell, I loved the guy.

"Sure" I said. "You got a pen?"

———

Some time passed. I forget exactly how long. But I woke up one morning to a phone call from Chris Ackerman, a rider who worked for Metal Mulisha. This, as it turned out, was the beginning of Chris' role as mediator between Brian and me.

"Hey, um . . . Larry?"

"Yeah?" I could tell he was nervous.

"Brian's really pissed at you, man. What happened?"

I tried to shake the cobwebs of sleep and whatever substances I'd consumed the previous night.

"Huh? I don't know what you're talking about."

"Well, something went down, because Brian says he doesn't want you to be part of Mulisha anymore."

What the fuck?!

I couldn't imagine what had happened; Chris must have been confused. Shit, Brian and I were still hanging out together, at least some of the time (although he wasn't partying as much as I was anymore) Hell, I'd even signed a new contract.

Uh-oh.

I forget which one of us made the call, but within a few hours, Brian and I were on the phone, engaged in a heated conversation. Brian said he was tired of carrying all the weight for the Metal Mulisha, and that he didn't think our partnership was an accurate representation of the roles we played within the company.

"I'm the one winning medals," he said. "I'm the one doing the X Games and the Gravity Games and all these other contests. I'm the one pulling in all the sponsors. It's not fair that I should have to give up half the money."

At first I didn't even know how to respond—I'd been completely blindsided by this whole development, so it took me a few minutes to begin fighting back. "You know what, bro? There wouldn't even be a Metal Mulisha if it weren't for me. And you know it."

"Yeah, well I'm carrying the load now, and it's not right for me to give you half of everything we make when it's my name they're buying."

"Are you serious?"

There was a pause.

"You're fucking right, I'm serious. I don't want to be in business with you anymore."

I felt dizzy, like my whole life had just been torn apart. It was like when a chick dumps you—only worse, because this was about my livelihood, too. It was about something I had created. I was pissed at myself for not having seen this coming, but I was also deeply hurt.

"Brian, this isn't just about medals or money. We're friends."

He didn't miss a beat. "Friends and business partners are two different things, aren't they?"

"I guess so."

After that conversation, I turned to my parents for help. Whatever else my father might have been in his life, at times he'd been a successful businessman. And my mom was sharp as anything, with a growing career at Aetna. I told them what had happened, and my father got really pissed, explained that only a few days earlier Brian had stopped by the winery and asked my parents for an infusion of cash to help the business. He'd also told my parents that I was totally fucked up on drugs (which was not completely untrue), and that Kella was ruining my life (also not completely untrue). Mom and Dad hated Kella as it was, and they naturally got all worked up over their conversation with Deegan. But when they found out that Brian wanted to kick me out of my own business, and that I had apparently signed some sort of document that would likely facilitate that arrangement, my parents quickly came to my defense.

"Something like this happened to me in one of my businesses," Dad said. "We'll get it fixed."

And we did. But it would take the better part of five years, during which time I was effectively locked out of my own company. Five years in which the Metal Mulisha advanced in fits and starts, sometimes making money, sometimes not. Five years in which I sank to the lowest depths imaginable.

There were times I wondered if I'd ever come back.

CHAPTER 14

Drug addicts and alcoholics will sometimes refer to "the lost weekend." I had a lost decade. For most of the 2000s a combination of staggering drug abuse, blind rage directed at my business partner (but unleashed on anyone in the vicinity at random times), and a still-undiagnosed brain injury rendered me almost clinically insane. In fact, that's exactly the term that doctors would eventually use, when I finally got the proper help. But man, would it take a long time to get there.

The shit I did during that period . . . it's hard to believe it was me sometimes. Much of my income stream dried up, and whatever money I did have went straight to my lawyers, as they fought to protect my interests in Metal Mulisha. It wasn't long before I was broke and virtually homeless (or at least rootless), thugging around with some of the gnarliest dudes you can imagine. Some of these guys were people I'd known since high school. A few had gone away and done time in prison, and now were back in the area. Many of them were hostile, angry guys—bordering on the outright psychotic—who lived either in the gang world or on its fringe. I never joined a gang myself, because on some level I understood the implications, and I didn't want anyone having that much control over my life. But I certainly could have gone that way. I lived mostly in the margins, fucked up out of my mind on hydrocodone, meth, heroin, Valium—whatever was available—carrying a gun in my waistband, sometimes engaging in bareknuckle underground fighting just to make a few hundred bucks, or to square debts on behalf of my buddies.

Total craziness.

In November 2002, my son was born. His name is Lynkin. Today I have primary custody of Lynkin and I think I'm a pretty good single dad. He's my closest friend and I love him with all my heart. But there's no way to sugarcoat the fact that I simply wasn't there for him during the first few years of his life. I'm embarrassed and pained to admit that, but it's the irrefutable truth. Kella and Lynkin lived for a while at my place in Temecula; then they moved to her place in Huntington Beach. I guess they figured there was no point in sticking around if I wasn't there anyway. Most of my friends hated Kella and did their best to make her feel uncomfortable, so she split for a while. Then she came back, and then she split again. Along the way we got married, but that had absolutely no bearing on our relationship. It was never much of a marriage.

Through no fault of anyone's but my own, I had no family at that time. My brothers were guys like Stan and Phil, and my boyhood buddy Connor. We all embraced a culture of drug abuse and fighting and hatred. The part of California where I grew up is recognized as something of a breeding ground for the separatist and white supremacy movements. Tom Metzger (no relation to Mike), a former grand dragon of the Ku Klux Klan, and the founder of the White Aryan Resistance, lived and ran his empire out of Fallbrook, which is only a few miles from Temecula. The WAR guys were all over our town when I was growing up; sometimes they'd come down to the high school and pass out literature in the parking lot. This was their recruitment style: blatant, open, and arrogant. But it resonated with a lot of kids I knew. Many of them came from dysfunctional families and suffered from low self-esteem or other issues (like drug abuse), so they were susceptible to propaganda. Sometimes they'd go up to Metzger's ranch and party, and soak up his bullshit about how the white race was under siege or whatever. Despite the fact that California is maybe the most racially diverse state in the country, our neighborhood was predominantly white. It didn't take much to get a lot of these kids riled up. They were looking for a fight anyway; they were looking for a cause. Hatred and separatism and bigotry were as good as any.

Despite the fact that I hung out with a lot of these kids growing up, I mostly stayed out of this shit for the longest time, mainly because I was too busy riding motorcycles to get involved. But I heard the drumbeat, and I suppose on some level it had an influence. I was more of a live-and-let-live kind of kid. But as a I got older, and my riding career and my business fell apart, and the drug use consumed me, and I spent more time in the world of gangs and pseudo-gangs, my moral compass began to break.

At the very least you'd have to say I was guilty by association. And where I was at that point in my life, I really didn't care. If people wanted to believe I was part of a racial movement, well, that didn't bother me. I was into the violence and drugs more than anything else. I mean, sometimes we'd go to a bar and there would be racial tension, and we'd take off on some blacks or Chicanos simply because they weren't white. But for me, it was just an excuse to hurt someone, to vent all that hostility and rage. Most of the time, though, we fought with other whites. Didn't matter to me in the least.

But I carry scars from those days that can't ever be totally wiped out. Some are emotional, some are physical, and some are . . . well . . . hidden. Lost in the collage of ink that adorns much of my body is a fairly small statement of how deep I sank in the depravity of that world. It makes me sick to think about it now. If not for fate and luck and God knows whatever else, I might have ended up in prison or dead. I'm not trying to rationalize what I did or who I was. I'm not blaming it on anyone else. I'm simply trying to be honest and candid. For me, it was all about hatred—fueled by ignorance and anger and the chemical destruction of my brain and body. I embraced the hating of a person not so much because of their ethnicity, but simply because they represented an opportunity to hate and to hurt. It gave me an excuse to be around a bunch of dudes that really didn't give a fuck and liked to smash up on people.

I wasn't thinking clearly. I lost who I was in my soul and my core, because both had been eaten by hatred. And that hatred was compounded by having been betrayed by my best friend and partner. Nothing mattered to me. Not my family or my new son or even life itself. I had always figured I'd live fast and die young anyway.

Connor lived up in Sun City, not far from Temecula. He had neighbor problems, a scrawny little white-boy tweaker who drove him nuts. I'm not sure how the fight started; probably didn't take much. Connor was a skinhead racist, but in many ways, he was an equal opportunity hater. Generally speaking, he was opposed to drug use, especially methamphetamine, so the steady flow of tweaker traffic really got on Connor's nerves. They fought about property lines and noise and who the fuck knows what else.

"I'm sick of this guy's bullshit," Connor said one day. "He keeps it up, I'm going to burn his fucking house down."

Connor had a legitimate job. He had a decent salary, a company car, full benefits. A normal nine-to-five guy, except that he was also a total fucking psycho, with no sense of irony or self-awareness, as evidenced by the fact that he was a drug user himself, although mostly Oxy and hydro, rather than meth. It was Connor who gave me my first handgun, a .380 to be flashed or used whenever the situation called for it. I got into a number of fights with Connor at my side; he was my friend, and if he had a troublesome neighbor, I'd help him put an end to the trouble.

"All right, dude. Let's fucking do it."

"I'm serious," Connor said.

I did not doubt him for a second.

So Connor came up with this mad-ass plan to torch the guy's house when he left for work one morning. I was spending a lot of time at Connor's place in those days, so I acted as lookout. I watched the guy kiss his girlfriend goodbye in the morning, get in his car, and drive away. Then I waited another half hour or so, until his chick left. And then I called Connor.

"They're gone," I said. "House is empty."

"Cool. On my way."

He came back home from work, grabbed a two-gallon plastic gas tank from the garage, walked across the street, and disappeared around the back of the house. A few minutes later, he reappeared, empty-handed.

"Let's go," he said as he walked into the house. "Can't be here when the cops come."

We went outside. Connor started the car. Then I realized I had left my backpack and some other shit in the house.

"I gotta go back in."

Connor seemed nervous. "Hurry up. And lock the door when you come out."

I went into the house, grabbed my backpack (which doubled as a traveling pharmacy) and my gun, and walked outside. As I locked the door—turning the bolt from the inside so that it would hammer closed automatically when I pulled it closed, I could hear Connor revving the engine of his car. And just as the door slammed shut, I turned around and saw him pulling away.

"You mother fucker!"

I guess he panicked, figuring that at any moment the tweaker's house was going to burst into flames and that the whole neighborhood would be crawling with fire trucks and cop cars. Still . . .

What the fuck, dude?

So there I was, locked out of the house, with a backpack full of drugs and a gun in my waistband, not more than a couple hundred feet from a house that had just been torched. I had to get out of there—fast.

I'd partied with some kids who lived in another house across the street, so I decided I'd try to duck in there. By now it was early afternoon and the house was usually active with some sort of party scene, so I rolled on over, didn't even knock on the door, just barged right in like nothing had happened. There were maybe a half dozen of them in the living room, getting loaded, watching TV, just hanging out.

"What's up, Larry?"

"Aw, nothing, man. Just stopping by."

"Yeah, cool. Come on in."

A few minutes of meaningless conversation followed. I wasn't really listening or paying attention; I was too busy looking out the window, waiting for plumes of smoke. And finally they came. At first, just little white streaks that looked as benign as a backyard barbecue. And then bigger, darker clouds, rising above the house, filling the air with smoke and stench.

"Oh, my God!" one of the girls shouted. "That house is on fire!"

They started to scramble. I pulled out my .380 and set it on a coffee table. That didn't really shock anyone, as most of these kids knew that I carried a gun—hell, some of them probably carried guns, too. But, then, very calmly, I raised the stakes.

"No one is calling anyone. And the door stays closed."

Everyone froze. I picked up the gun, rolled it around in my hand for a moment or two, then put it in back in my waistband. The room fell silent. Everyone got the point. For the next half hour or so, until the fire department arrived and went to work, we basically sat there and watched the tweaker's house burn down. And when the cops came poking around over the next couple days, knocking on doors and asking questions, no one said a word. (We never did get caught, although Connor would eventually do several years in prison on other charges unrelated to arson). Every kid detained in that house held his mud, not out of any sense of pride or solidarity or friendship, but surely out of plain old fear. Some of them weren't exactly law-abiding citizens themselves, but they understood now that Connor and I were on a whole different level. You torch a guy's house and you send a pretty clear message.

In this case, the message was, "Don't fuck with us, because we are completely out of our minds."

―――――――――

Believe it or not, I had a clean record. Still do, in fact. Despite all of the drinking and drugging, smuggling shit across borders, being under federal surveillance for alleged gang activity, driving under the influence, buying and selling narcotics—despite all of that, and the myriad opportunities to be tossed in jail, I have never even spent a single night behind bars. And it wasn't for lack of trying. Looking back on it, I think a part of me actually wanted to go to jail; stupid as it sounds, I wanted that rep, and the street cred that comes with it. I didn't fear going inside; shit, I would have known half the guys in there. But I would have gotten caught up in the politics, for sure. Few people do time on their own. I had a lot of skinhead buddies and I would have felt compelled to join their ranks in prison. And the truth is, once you're in the system, you don't really ever come out. You're in for life—even on the outside.

But I avoided all of that. I escaped, and I have no way to explain it, except to say that someone up there must have been looking out for me. Either that or just plain old dumb luck.

Anyway, as one of the few guys in our circle of friends who did not have a criminal record, I was sometimes appointed the role of gladiator. Here's the way it worked: if there was a beef between members of our pack (and, again, we were not an actual "gang," although we frequently behaved like one; some of these guys were like the nomads of the gang world, guys not officially affiliated with the traditional gangs, but so nasty and cold-blooded that they'd get recruited by the gangs once in a while if they needed a particularly brutal or risky act carried out), of another pack, or simply between one of our guys and one of their guys, it would be settled the old fashioned way: with bare knuckles in a back alley or field or garage. This was preferable to guns or knives, of course. The problem was that often the people involved could not risk the possibility of getting pinched by the cops. A dude out on parole picks up a felony assault charge and he's going away for a very long time.

So it wasn't unusual for someone to recruit me on their behalf.

"Need you to be my hands, brother," he'd say. "I can't afford to get caught. Got two strikes already. One more and I'm doing life."

My initial reaction was usually something along the lines of "Ah, fuck!" followed by, "Do I have to?"

"Well, no, but if you don't smash up on him, we're going to smash up on you. What's it going to be?"

Not much of a choice, really. It's so strange to look back on this now. Like I said, I wasn't a fighter growing up. I was a fairly peaceful fuck-up who liked to ride motorcycles. But I became an adrenaline junkie; and then a regular junkie. And then I combined the two and became, well, the kind of guy who finds himself in a field outside Temecula, peeling his shirt off and trading punches with another dude four or five inches taller and fifty pounds heavier. And all around us are guys from both groups, cheering and cursing and laughing, and betting a shit pile of cash on the outcome.

"Make us proud, Dude."

"Don't let us down."

The first few times I'd feel like I was going to puke before the fight. The anticipation was always the worst. But like anything else, you get used to it after a while. Once the first punch was thrown, it was all adrenaline and survival. I wasn't like Phil or Stan, obviously, but I got to be pretty good with my fists. Won most of my fights, routinely beat guys into submission, and pocketed a percentage of the betting pool for my efforts. Basically it was like human cock-fighting, and if at first it was something I did only out of obligation or threat of bodily harm, it soon became something I did basically for sport; for fun.

And for money.

It didn't happen weekly or even monthly—bareknuckle fighting is highly illegal, after all, and it's hard to stage a big match quietly—but I did have many fights, some of which were captured on video and sold on the black market. I was a professional motorcycle rider with a name, and so my participation brought a little extra value to the exercise. If I was short on cash (which was most of the time), I could go out and make a few hundred bucks by beating someone up. I'd usually get hurt in the process, but I didn't care. Pain was irrelevant. In fact, I sort of liked the pain. I liked getting hurt. On some level, I suppose, I felt like I deserved to be hurt.

━━━━━

I needed money and I needed pills.

I needed money to buy the pills that would feed my drug habit and keep me from getting sick; and I needed the pills to make money. I couldn't fight often enough to earn a living, so hustling Oxy became my primary job. The ostensibly legal channels through which I had previously acquired much of my supply had all but dried up. Following a previous trip to rehab, I had actually paid a visit to Dr. Kevorkian and piously ended our relationship.

"Check it out, Doc. I'm through with this shit. If I ever come back and ask you for pills, don't give them to me. Okay?"

"You sure about this."

"Absolutely."

So, of course, I ended up back in Dr. Kevorkian's office, sick, strung out, begging for opiates. And you know what? That mother fucker turned me down.

"A deal is a deal," he said. "Don't ever come back here."

Illicit drugs are always available, especially if you know your way around the street. But I needed enough drugs to provide a revenue stream as well. So I began making regular runs across the border to Tijuana, where you could get almost anything for a fraction of the cost in the states. If you knew the right pharmacy, all you had to do was walk in, ask for the right person, pay the right price, and you could leave with a hundred Valium or Vicodin. I'd keep some for myself and sell the rest. But without Dr. Kevorkian's assistance, it became increasingly difficult to balance the books (so to speak).

More money was needed, and obtained, by any means necessary.

In 2004 I began making regular trips to the central part of the state, primarily to Bakersfield and Taft—dusty, dirty little places, heavily into the drug trade—with ample opportunity to make money in non-traditional ways. Stan had hooked up with some dude who was involved in trafficking stolen goods—home theater systems, stereo speakers, and other electronics that had somehow been diverted on their way from warehouses in China to retailers in the United States. Mostly cheap shit that they could sell out of the back of a van or truck while cruising around town. Just pull up to a street corner, where the clientele isn't likely to ask any probing questions, roll down the window, and make your sales pitch.

"Hey, Bro . . . you need a new CD player for your car?"

I hopped onto that bandwagon for a while. It was easy money, hustling speakers to meth-dealing dudes who wanted surround sound in their trailers. Depending on how tweaked out the customer was, you could make as little as five bucks on a transaction, or as much as fifteen hundred. Let the buyer beware, right? And if the buyer was spracked out of his mind, he didn't often argue. You could take him for whatever he had in his wallet.

Eventually we began spending more time in Taft, and our interests and efforts expanded beyond the peddling of crappy electronics. We basically developed a strong-armed racket to capitalize on the heavy drug trade—primarily crystal meth—going through town. It was during this period that I actually developed an intense meth addiction, in part because it was readily available, but also because it was becoming so difficult to acquire sufficient supplies of opiates—hydro and Vicodin and Demerol. Crazy as it sounds, in the back of my mind, I still harbored the possibility of getting sober, and I figured it would be easier down the road to kick meth rather than opiates.

In the world of addiction, that is what is commonly known as a rationalization. In my case, it was born of delusion and an increasing detachment from reality.

When it came to meth, we were thugs, not dealers, the former being a far safer way to make a living than trying to interfere with the various cartels that controlled the flow of traffic; we simply collected a "commission" (for lack of a better term) from the small-time tweakers in town. If we found out some chump was peddling meth on his own, we'd go to his house, kick the door down, and take his money. If they wanted to do business in Taft, they'd have to give us a piece of the action.

Protection money, I guess you'd call it.

It was dangerous, highly illegal work, but somehow we managed to avoid being arrested or killed. But we came close on numerous occasions. (I later discovered that one of our comrades was also a police informant, which no doubt helped keep the heat off our backs.) In all honesty, though, money was only one motivating factor. Mostly I did it for the adrenaline fix—for the pure, unadulterated thrill of it. I got off on the lifestyle, the intimidation—where you can walk into a place and know that nobody is going to mess with you, and you can basically take whatever you want. It's not the kind of thing you do in a normal state of mind, of course. It's all tied into the drug use and (for me) the brain damage. Stan and I would stay up for seven, eight, nine days at a time, doing meth and busting through doors. When you're on a jag like that, there is no rational thinking. There is only animal impulse.

Looking back on it, I guess you could say I was at war with myself. I was so disgruntled with the way things had gone with my life and career. Then you mix in the drugs and the injuries and the business going bad, and you end up with this incredibly volatile person. I had so much hatred inside of me. The thing I regret most is the pain I caused my parents. My dad had pretty much written me off, and I would get reports back from people that my mom was calling them, and that she was really distraught. She'd cry and beg them for help.

"I can't sleep at night," she'd tell them. "I'm afraid the phone is going to ring and there will be someone on the other end telling me that my son is gone."

It was a legitimate concern.

Not that I cared.

Everything snowballed in Taft. We stayed up there for probably a couple months, pushing up against people, getting in fights, taking whatever we wanted, smoking speed day and night. Stan was like a god up there. Everyone knew him, both as a legitimate cage fighter and as a force to be feared on the street. If you rolled up with Stan, you had instant validation and credibility. Stan was a seriously intimidating, frightening dude, especially if he was roided up (his weight would balloon to 230 pounds or more, giving him the appearance of a human cinder block). Together we were like a deranged duo. Two screamingly fucked up, dangerous guys. I was a veteran drug addict by this time, but meth took me to a whole different level in terms of aggressiveness and paranoia. Not only wasn't I afraid of fighting, I actively sought confrontation and violence. Meth actually provoked fits of extreme violence; it made me want to kill people.

It turned me into an animal. I'd be sitting there in a tweaked-out stupor, not having slept in three or four days, and I'd envision getting in my car and driving down to Temecula, walking up to Deegan's house and literally snapping his neck with my bare hands. I thought about that. I wanted to do it. And I could have done it. Not because I was big enough and strong enough, but because I was that crazy.

Our time in Taft was a maelstrom of violence and extortion and drug use. Meeting this person and that person, bouncing from place to place, party to party, job to job. The big fish eating the little fish, as Phil used to say. One of the most bizarre characters I got to know in Taft was a guy named J.D., a total fucking crazy-ass gangster. This guy was no poser or interloper. He was a killer; had gotten out of prison just a few months earlier. We started hanging at J.D.'s place every night, smoking speed for a few hours to pre-game, then hitting the streets, wild-eyed and crazy, thugging till our wallets were full. Then we'd do it all over again the next day.

You do outrageous, crazy shit when you're in this state of mind, like driving from Taft to Tijuana, cranked to the eyeballs, just to break up the routine.

It was J.D.'s birthday, as I recall. We were hanging out, trading war stories, and at some point, I started taking about all the trips I'd made to Mexico.

"Yeah, I heard it's wild," J.D. said.

"Dude, what do you mean, 'You've heard?'"

J.D. shrugged. "Never been there, man."

I couldn't believe it! How could anyone living in central or southern California not have made at least one trip to Tijuana? Especially if you were a gangster?

"Oh, fuck, man . . . we gotta get you down there. It's off the hook! You can get prostitutes, drugs, anything you want. Won't hardly cost you a buck."

J.D.'s eyes lit up. "No fuckin' way, dude!"

"I'm serious. You want to go?"

J.D. nodded. The only problem was that Tijuana was about three hundred miles away. A straight shot down I-5, maybe five hours, give or take, depending on traffic around L.A. Easy enough for most people. Not so easy if you've been up doing meth for days on end. Nevertheless, we piled into Stan's car and headed on down the freeway.

The first thing I did when we arrived, naturally, was hit up one of my favorite pharmacies. I knew the area well, had a good working relationship with some of the folks there, and after a little while, we walked out with a bunch of painkillers and Valium. We ate a handful of pills and the rest I stowed away. Took a little pocket knife, cut a hole in the tongue of my boot, and stuffed my pills in there, along with a small bag of meth.

"If you got any cash," I said, "put most of it in your sock. Don't carry more than a few bucks in your pockets."

We drove around for a while, cruising slowly through the shadiest neighborhoods, looking at all the whores and junkies and low-rent gangsters, trying to figure out how we were going to spend our money, when suddenly I got an idea. In Mexico, it seemed, every head shop sold an assortment of glass pipes. And you could buy them literally for pennies.

"You know what we should do?" I said. "We should buy up a bunch of these speed pipes and bring them back home. Shit, everyone there is making pipes out of air fresheners or whatever. These fuckers are already made. We could sell them to the tweakers in Taft for five bucks apiece."

Stan and J.D. smiled.

Before long we had parked our car and found a conduit for our business venture, a hard little Mexican guy who led us deeper and deeper into the bowels of the city's red light district (which is much of Tijuana, come to think of it). We walked down an alleyway, in a part of town that felt incredibly unsafe, where drug deals and other illicit activity went on right out in the open, overlooked by tough and nasty looking guys who clearly were not accustomed to seeing Americans in their midst. Not here. Not in this neighborhood. I mean, we should not have been there, but all three of us were so gnarly at the time, and so out of our fucking minds, that no one messed with us. We marched through clumps of would-be gangbangers, kids waving broomsticks and probably carrying guns and knives. I'm sure when we first approached they were ready to jump us, but for some reason they reconsidered. Maybe it was our size—three thickly muscled men, each over six feet tall and weighing more than two hundred pounds. Maybe it was the tattoos. More likely it was something less obvious, a vibe thrown off by three guys who clearly were out of their out minds. We weren't intimidated in the least. We simply did not give a fuck. Whatever Tijuana had to offer, we were ready. Or so we thought.

It took a lot to freak me out, but there were sights on that particular trip that have stayed with me for years. We walked down a corridor between rows of shabby apartment buildings that looked like the worst kind of American roadside motels—the sort that have been taken over by public assistance, with cracked windows and paint peeling off the outer walls. Many of the doors were open, providing a glimpse into the lives of its occupants. There were cribs and screaming children and a steady stream of sweaty, slovenly men. Working women of indeterminate age turning tricks in front of their babies. Dope being sold on the sidewalk. People pissing and puking in public. In general, a little corner of hell.

In one apartment there was a hole in the middle of the floor. Just an open drain, without a cover, right in the center of the living room. God knows how it got there or what was being dumped into it, or where it was going. A woman walked to the drain, carrying something in her hand. We made eye contact. She seemed unfazed, just pulled up her dress and squatted over the drain. After a couple moments, I could see what she was holding: a spray bottle of some sort, filled with blue liquid. I was transfixed and horrified. She crouched further and began spraying herself, shooting Windex or whatever the hell it was up into her crotch.

Holy fucking Christ!

Never had I seen a more effective public service announcement for discouraging the patronizing of prostitutes. Instinctively I reached for my own dick, as if trying to protect it from whatever might be wafting out of the room.

A couple doors down was another chick smoking speed out of a light bulb. This was more up my alley. We cruised on in, and she immediately gave her boyfriend the boot because she wanted to get busy. He got kind of pissed but eventually walked out, cursing under his breath in Spanish. We smoked some speed, and then J.D. started getting that look in his eye, like he wanted a little action, so he and this chick got going, started groping each other, and me and Stan and his contact hit the road on our glass pipe mission.

We wound up at a dodgy little compound at the back of the city. For some reason the place made me nervous. Probably just the paranoia that comes with going sleepless for two or three days, coupled with having just smoked a shitload of low-grade and perhaps contaminated meth. Whatever the reason, as Stan handled negotiations for the pipes, I felt a sudden urge to get the hell out of there.

"You got this, dude? I need to bounce."

He nodded.

I walked outside and around the back of the building. The timing was unbelievable, for not more than ten seconds after I walked out, the cops—*federales!*—burst through the front door. I actually saw them kicking it down.

Ah, fuck! Stan is so fucking fucked!

And we were fucked by extension, since Stan had the car keys. From a short distance away, I could see them with guns drawn, pulling people out of the building, throwing them up against the squad cars, shaking them down. Some were cuffed; others were given a shove and sent on their way. There was nothing I could do. Stan was on his own.

I doubled back to find J.D., but I was lost and vibed and generally still in cuckooville from all the speed. I kept my little pocketknife handy, since traveling solo greatly increased the likelihood of getting jumped. Eventually I found J.D., who was just finishing up with the pro. Outside, getting all riled up, was the chick's boyfriend, who had now recruited a small army of his buddies to deal with J.D. and me.

"Yo, J.D., we gotta roll."

He tossed me a hard look, reminding me that when it came to being a badass, J.D. was on a whole different level.

"I'm fucking kickin' it here, man. Leave me alone."

"Come on, Dude. This place is fucked up! There's a gang outside, chicks are squirting Windex into their pussies, and I think Stan just got rolled."

That last part got his attention.

"Huh? Where?"

"Come on. I'll show you."

We hadn't gone very far before another cop car rolled up on us, with two *federales* inside. They began berating us and screaming at us in a mixture of Spanish and broken English, demanding that we empty our pockets. I'd been to Mexico often enough to know that you can buy your way out of almost any jam. Especially in Tijuana, the cops weren't really interested in fighting crime; they were interested in fattening their own wallets. The trick was to remain calm while they went about the business of extortion.

One of the cops pushed J.D. up against a wall, dug into his pocket, and pulled out three little pills.

"Five years in jail!" he said. "*Cinco anos!*"

J.D. just scoffed.

"Fuck you."

The cops pushed him around a little, kept trying to scare him, which obviously didn't work, and after a while we got down to business. The cops really didn't want to bring us into jail, for that would only create paperwork and cut into their extortion time for the night; nor did they want to beat us up and steal our money—although they could have done that, I suspect they knew it would have been a fight, and explanations would have been required at the precinct house. No, they wanted to keep it simple. So they told us they'd let us go—if we paid them five hundred dollars.

J.D. gave them what he had: three hundred in cash.

No good, they said. Five hundred or we were going to jail.

Then they turned their attention to me. They searched my pockets, found my knife, and began laughing.

Deadly weapon, they said. Five years for me, too. Now they wanted five hundred dollars from me, as well.

"Fuck you. I'm not giving a fucking penny."

And so it went, back and forth, the cops threatening and demanding cash, me refusing to play along, being obstinate and disrespectful, despite knowing that if they found the pills and speed in my shoe, they really would haul my ass into jail. I didn't care.

"Fuck you," I said . . . again and again, until finally they tossed us both into the back of the cop car.

"Son of a bitch!" J.D. said. "We're going to jail."

"Yeah, maybe, Dude. But at least we're going together!"

J.D. did not laugh.

We drove around for maybe a half hour, and in that time, I got to see exactly how the city of Tijuana operates. The cops had informants on every street corner—guys who were selling drugs and pushing prostitutes—and they'd repeatedly roll up to the informants, find out what was happening, and then use the information to make arrests and extort money. And sometimes they'd just flat-out strong-arm people: pulling wallets out of pockets and taking cash, ripping necklaces off of necks, watches from wrists. They were incredibly efficient and arrogant. As far as I could tell, there was absolutely no difference between the criminals and the cops in Tijuana—except that the cops had badges and could do whatever they wanted without fear of reprisal. I'd been all over the world and seen a lot of bad behavior on the part of law enforcement, but it was hard to imagine a more corrupt police force than the one in Tijuana.

Incredibly, while we were cruising around, we passed Stan walking on the sidewalk.

"That's our buddy," I yelled. "Pull over!"

So they did. And immediately began trying to put the squeeze on Stan, telling him that if he didn't come up with the five hundred dollars, his two friends were going to jail.

"Don't give them anything," I said. "Fuck these guys."

Stan nodded. "Okay."

"Just follow us," I said. "We'll take care of it downtown."

So Stan got his car, which was parked only a short distance away, and followed the cops. But we didn't go to the precinct house or to jail, or anywhere else affiliated with the police department. Instead, we drove to a gated parking lot with a twenty-foot-high chain link fence circling the perimeter. Another cop car soon followed. The gate locked behind us. There was only one way in, one way out. Nowhere to run, nowhere to hide.

Oh, shit . . . they're going to kill us.

It did seem possible. And still, I did not care.

Knowing that J.D. was broke and weary of my obstinacy, the *federales* began bargaining with Stan. To my surprise (and disappointment), he seemed relatively open to the idea.

"I'm fucking serious, Stan," I said. "Don't give these assholes any money. I would rather go to jail than let them rip us off."

There was more conversation. The cops backpedaled a bit, said they'd let us go if we gave them our cell phones.

"Fuck you!" It was Stan, all puffed up and suddenly down for a fight. "You mother-fuckers ain't getting our cell phones, and you ain't getting five hundred dollars. You ain't getting shit!"

For a few moments there, it got super intense. One of the cops drew his gun. There was shouting back and forth, an indecipherable mix of Spanish and English. They were beyond pissed, and if they wanted to murder us, they surely could have. If they wanted to beat us, well, that might have been a different story. Either way, they came to the sudden realization that we were more trouble than we were worth. There were smaller and easier fish to fry out there on the streets, so why waste time and energy and bullets on three crazy tweaked out gringos? The cops huddled together. Then one of them waved a hand dismissively and spit into the dirt.

"Vete a la verga!"

(Get the fuck outta here!)

And just like that, the standoff ended. We got into Stan's car and drove away, watching the cops recede in the rearview mirror.

Ten minutes passed in stunned silence as we cruised out of town and headed for the border. Only then did I start to wonder how the hell Stan had ended up out in the street. Last time I'd seen him, he'd been on the verge of getting pinched.

"What happened?" I asked. "You bribe the cops?"

Stan laughed. Turned out he was in the bathroom when the raid went down. He heard the cops busting down doors and hid behind some boxes in a little broom closet until the commotion ended. They never even saw him!

"No fuckin' way, bro! That is gnarly!" Then I remembered something. "Guess we're fucked on our little pipe deal, though, huh?"

Stan threw his head back, laughed ominously.

"Not exactly. Soon as the cops left, I took everything."

"Oh, Stan. You are the man!"

So there we were, with a car full of paraphernalia, motoring toward the border. Stan had tossed his shit, J.D.'s pills had been confiscated, so they presumed we were drug free at the time. We cruised through customs without a problem and drove on through the night, five hours of dark, empty highway ahead of us.

And then came the crash.

Not the vehicular kind, but the kind that comes when you've been up for three days, spracked out of your mind, chewing pills and smoking speed and playing dice with whacked-out corrupt Mexican cops. After all of that comes the crash.

For the next hour we rode on quietly. Occasionally Stan or J.D. would bitch about feeling like crap, and wishing they had just a hit of something to make the trip go by faster.

That's when I reached into my shoe.

"Oh, boys . . . look what I've got."

I pulled out the little bag of meth and waved it around.

"Bro! Are you kidding me?! That is awesome!!"

And so we broke out one of the pipes and torched the meth, and smoked until the exhaustion melted away, and the highway grew shorter and smaller. Sick and twisted as it might have been, I felt like a fucking hero.

CHAPTER 15

The road back from hell was far from smooth. Most addicts find the journey to be something of a roller-coaster ride, and I was no different. But you get nowhere until you take the first step, and mine came in late 2004. One of my closest buddies and riding partners, Trigger Gumm, had somehow gotten word that I was up in Taft, getting into all kinds of trouble. So he did what no one else had considered: he tried to take me home.

Here's the thing about Trig that you might not realize if you just happened to run into him at a restaurant or a shopping mall, or watch him being interviewed. The dude has this eternally youthful choirboy look to him that is wildly deceiving. Trig is nearly a decade older than I am, but he's significantly smaller and has had the same soft features as long as I've known him. He's smart and approachable and a genuinely decent man.

But he's also one of the gnarliest people I've ever known, with a hard-earned reputation for fighting and drugging that, at one time, equaled or exceeded my own. Trig grew up in Montana and then San Clemente, and for a while ran with some serious gangsters. He and Christian Fletcher were like my elders when I first met them, guys who pushed the envelope twenty-four seven. They could ride and fight and party, they got the hottest chicks, and they did not give a fuck what anyone thought about them. Although they never asked for the job, they were my role models. I watched and I learned; I listened to the crazy stories about their skinhead buddies going to war. It all seemed so . . . alluring. Intentionally or not, I was indoctrinated, and eventually I surpassed them on the journey to self-destruction.

Those guys pulled out of the death spiral long before I did—maybe because they're older. And Trig . . . well, he came to my rescue. Or tried to anyway. In the end, you have to save yourself. But it helps to know that someone else cares.

We bumped into each other under the oddest of circumstances. I was hanging out with Stan, planning the day's business, when my dog managed to get out of the house. Now, I loved this dog. He was a pit bull I'd rescued in the parking lot of an abandoned Kmart. The dog was my constant companion; he went everywhere with me, so when he ran out into the street, I chased after him as quickly as I could. As I ran down the driveway, the dog scurried out into traffic and under the front end of an oncoming car.

"No!"

Stan was right behind me and we both flipped out. The car did not stop; didn't even slow down, actually. Miraculously, the dog emerged unscathed. Somehow the car must have run right over him cleanly, and he suffered only a few cuts and bruises. Nevertheless, we were enraged. Why were they driving so fast? And who hits a dog without at least stopping to see if the animal is okay?

We jumped into our car and gave chase, fully intending to beat the driver within an inch of his life. But then the strangest thing happened. As we pulled up to a traffic light, a different car pulled up alongside us. A big, black Cadillac. The driver rolled down his window, and there, behind the steering wheel, was my buddy Trig.

Whoaaaaa . . .

He smiled.

"Hey, Link. You know how long I've been looking for you?"

Almost too disoriented to speak, I just shook my head.

"I've been driving around up here for two fuckin' days, man."

He paused briefly, then looked at Stan.

"You do what you gotta do, man. But this guy's coming with me. I'm taking him home."

I laughed.

Home? Where was that? *What* was that? I had a house back in Temecula. I had a two-year-old son I barely knew and a wife I did not love. Was that home? I honestly did not know where I belonged, but I had started to grow weary of the life I was leading. Despite the fact that we had drifted apart, Trig was one of my oldest and best friends. I was moved by the fact that he was willing to drive up to Taft and try to pull me out of this shithole. He cared enough to do that. I still don't even know why.

I looked at Trig.

"Okay. Sounds good to me."

We ended up driving back to my place, where Trig and Stan had a fairly heated conversation, one that could have resulted in Stan snapping Trig's neck, but instead ended with Trig handing over a fistful of cash. Only then would Stan permit me to leave. Misery loves company, you know? But even misery has its price.

━━━━━

The next few years passed by with the staccato rhythm of rehab and relapse. I began to notice, though, that neither sobriety nor fame could bring peace. I wasn't ready to make the necessary changes in my life, hadn't stopped associating with people of questionable character, hadn't figured out why I hated myself so much, or why I continued to self-sabotage.

Incredibly, some people kept giving me second, third, and fourth chances. People like Steve Van Doren, who would continue to offer financial and emotional support, taking me on tours and to shows, even when I didn't deserve it. Or my mom, who went deep into her own savings to help me fight a protracted legal battle over Metal Mulisha. And Jon Freeman, who called me up one day in 2005 and asked if I wanted to be part of a Crusty Demons tour in Australia and New Zealand. The highlight would be a single night in which we would try to shatter several world distance records on various bikes.

Originally I was not supposed to be part of this event, but when Seth Enslow injured his ankle, a replacement was needed. I got the call, which frankly surprised the shit out of me. But I had some sober time in and I'd been doing a fair amount of riding. Compared to recent years, I was in good shape. So I accepted the offer. And on May 5, 2005, at Queensland Raceway in Ipswich, Australia, I cleared 255.4 feet to set a world record for the 250cc class. The event was known as the Crusty Demons Night of World Records, and that's exactly what it was. We set a total of six records that evening, in front of an insanely appreciative crowd. My parents were there to see it. So was my son. It was one of the best nights of my life. I felt totally focused and dialed-in. I felt strong and healthy—like a kid.

But it didn't last. I fell off the wagon in Australia, started using again, and before long found myself crawling again through the shit-stained squalor of addict alley, running off to Mexico for more Oxy or Valium; sometimes I'd take fifteen, twenty pills in a single dose—that's how much of a tolerance I'd built up. And heroin, of course. Every addict talks about hitting bottom. I've been so low so many times that I'm not even sure bottom exists, but black tar heroin got me close. I used regularly for a while with my friends "HoBag" and "Big Trav." Through them I got to know a Chicano dude from Lake Elsinore named Sammy the Heroin Dealer.

We'd go over to Sammy's apartment, which was located in a complex right behind the police station, and score as much dope as we needed. But every trip was an exercise in disgust. For one thing, Sammy lived with his seventy-year-old mother and his smack-addled prostitute of a girlfriend. Sammy was six feet tall and weighed about ninety pounds. He was basically a walking, talking corpse, with his hair pulled back into a greasy ponytail, and bruises and abscesses and broken veins all over his arms. His girlfriend was nearly as repulsive, and yet she'd routinely turn tricks to pay the bills. You can imagine the clientele. We'd be sitting there in the kitchen, doing our deal, when there'd be a knock at the door. Ol' Sammy would answer, talk to the guy for a minute, they'd exchange a few bucks, and then Sammy would give the order.

"Take this dude in the back so he can cum up real quick, ok?"

His chick would nod, stump out her cigarette, hack up a wad of phlegm, and go to work.

All addicts find the lines of supply choked up once in a while, and so it was with me and Sammy. He had trouble getting enough dope, and I found myself getting sicker and sicker. Same with HoBag and Big Trav. Finally Sammy called and said he'd found an acquaintance who could hook us up. He gave us the address—a trailer park—and we agreed to meet there. It was the day before Mother's Day 2006.

Our heroin dealer was a woman in her fifties, heavyset and weathered. Her trailer was musty and dark and decorated with hundreds of little porcelain statuettes. Angels, mostly. Whole place creeped me out, but I was too fucking dope sick to care. I just wanted to tie off and end the pain. We all did.

"Here we go!" Sammy shouted as he emptied a little plastic bag and began cooking. Soon he had a spoon filled with liquid; HoBag, Big Trav, Sammy's chick, and the old lady drug dealer went at it like a pack of wild dogs on a carcass, pushing each other aside and drawing smack into their needles all at the same time. A communal trough.

I was about to dive in, but found myself hesitating. Already queasy from withdrawal, I felt the urge to vomit.

"What's the problem?" Sammy asked.

"I don't know, man . . . all those fuckin' needles in there."

"Ah, don't worry. Long as you wash them with bleach, it's no problem." He laughed. "Sharing needles ain't no big thing. I do it all the time."

For some reason, that was not a persuasive argument.

All of a sudden, Sammy jumped to his feet, handed the syringe to his old lady, and shouted, "You gotta hit me!"

Apparently Sammy's veins had receded so badly that he could no longer find an adequate spot on his arms or legs to insert the needle, so he needed another entry point. As his old lady took the syringe, Sammy balled his hands into fists and closed his eyes. He braced himself. Sammy's chick took the needle and drove it into his neck. Sammy let out a little groan and sank to the floor. Sufficiently doped, but starting to nod off, he held up a hand and offered to reciprocate.

"Need me to do you?"

The chick waved him off. "Nah, I got it."

And with that, she hammered the needle into her own jugular vein and pushed the contents into her body.

Within a few minutes, I was the only one in the room who wasn't loaded. As dopesick as I was, I just couldn't bring myself to dip into that pool of Hep C sitting on the table. Instead, I asked the old lady dealer for a little ball of smack—to go—and gave her a few extra bucks. She must have liked me, because she also threw in a basket filled with scented bars of soap.

"Give these to your mother tomorrow," she said. "She'll appreciate it."

"Uh . . . yeah. Thanks."

We were just about to leave when a pair of cop cars rolled up outside. There was a knock at the door. The old lady dealer sprang into action like a pro, grabbing all the drugs and paraphernalia in the room and stuffing them under her shirt. She ran into a back room as the police broke through the front door.

For the next hour we sat there quietly as the cops turned the trailer inside out. They searched each one of us. They checked drawers and mattresses and toilets. They looked everywhere and found absolutely nothing. You could tell they were pissed. Here they had a trailer full of people clearly smacked out of their minds, and yet no evidence of drugs.

"Where is the fucking dope?!" one of the cops yelled.

We all shrugged.

Eventually the cops gave up and left, without so much as an apology: *"Oops, our bad. Sorry. Thought we had the bust."*

After they left, the old lady started snickering.

"Works every time."

"What works?" I asked.

"This . . ."

And with that, she pulled up her shirt to expose her midsection. There, in the middle of what should have been her stomach, was what looked like a second set of butt cheeks.

"Few years ago my old man and me both got shot," she explained. "Fuckers killed him. But I made it. Bullet went in the back and came out the front. A .357. Fuckin' cannon. Left me like this." She ran her hands over the cheeks. "Awful, huh?"

I was speechless. Of all the horrid shit I'd seen in my life, this was right near the top. Or bottom, as the case may be.

"But I'll tell you—it comes in handy sometimes."

She then pulled the cheeks apart, revealing a large hole, almost like a pocket in the middle of her belly. She reached into the pocket and began pulling out everything she'd hidden: the syringes, spoons, dope . . . everything.

"I could put half the house in here," she said, cackling like a crazy old witch.

She handed me the ball of smack. I took it, put it my pocket, and walked out the door, sober and sick, but numb to the core. I shot up when I got home. And again the next morning. I can still see the look on my mom's face when I saw her that day and tried to wish her a Happy Mother's Day, slurring my words and stumbling across the room. She couldn't hide the disappointment, and the utter bewilderment when I tried to give her the basket of soap. She couldn't hide the sadness and despair.

And I hated myself for it.

═══════════

I cleaned up again, started riding, getting in shape. Opportunities came my way, some of which I grabbed, some of which slipped away. Mike Metzger and I squared up against each other in a cool Discovery Channel reality show called *Biker Build-Off*. I got introduced to a guy named Martin Trejo from Mandalay Entertainment; he and his brother worked hard for a while on trying to figure out a way to script my life and sell it as a reality television series or maybe even a feature film. Hard as I'd tried to wreck my image, apparently it was still marketable. They were good people, and while I understand it's a business and they were trying to make a buck, they also seemed genuinely interested in working with me. People like that come into your life sometimes, when you least expect it; you have to be willing to open your eyes and your arms.

I started going to a lot of big parties and events, because that's the how the entertainment industry works. You shake a lot of hands, make small talk, and try to get people to buy what you're selling, whatever that might be. I just tried to be a fairly clean and sober version of who I was. One day in late 2006 or early 2007, I found myself at a party at Donald Trump's Mar-A-Lago Club in Palm Beach, Florida. I was introduced to a woman who seemed like one of the smartest and most genuine people I'd ever met. We hit it off instantly and soon developed a friendship that became more than just a friendship.

I had pretty much given up on the entire concept of love. In fact, I'm not sure I'd ever loved anyone before I met this woman. I'm up front about everything; when I meet someone, I don't try to hide who I am or what I've done. *This is me, this is the deal.* In the case of this particular person, honesty and candor were particularly important, since she was a prominent figure, someone easily recognized and often trailed by paparazzi. So I told her early on about some of the shit that I'd done, and the people with whom I had associated. I told her that in my ignorant and drug-addled, hate-filled past, I had behaved in ways that caused me shame.

She said it didn't matter. None of it.

"I know who you are now. You're a good person."

She had nothing to gain by developing a relationship with me; in fact, she had a lot to lose. But she did it anyway, and her family came along as part of the package. They embraced me and took me in and cared for me in a way no one ever had (outside of my mom and dad, of course). It was the first time in my life that I really ever felt loved by anybody; this woman cared for me in an amazing way, and she was the best friend I could have ever had. She was a blessing that came into my life when I needed it most, and she and her family remain extraordinarily close to me even now. She was with me the first time I had a seizure. We were on a road trip, driving from Baltimore to Philadelphia. She was behind the wheel; I was in the passenger seat. I remember talking. And then I remember waking up. My shoulder ached and my mouth hurt. My tongue was swollen. I felt dizzy.

"Are you okay?" she asked. "You got quiet all of a sudden. And then you started shaking."

"I don't remember."

She nodded, gave me her hand. She seemed scared. I figured it was nothing. I was wrong.

Sometimes I'd call her up, just to talk, and after a few minutes, she'd interrupt me.

"Larry, you're not making any sense. I don't know what you're saying."

Then I'd snap out of it, like I was in a trance or something. "I'm sorry. I don't know what I was saying, either."

And that was the beginning of an insanely rough period in which I was not on drugs, and yet totally confused and disoriented—and seemingly loaded. I should qualify that. There were times I used, but for the most part, my drug use at this point was limited to a prescription non-narcotic pain reliever (obtained legally, just for the record) called Tramadol. I'd been taking it for years to deal with the fallout from various injuries, as well as the chronic headaches I'd suffered ever since the accident on the set of *Triple X*. Tramadol was supposed to be safe and effective; it is commonly prescribed to patients who either cannot tolerate opiates or should not take opiates for reasons related to dependency or addiction. It wasn't until 2008 that I finally ran into a neurologist who told me that while Tramadol is usually safe, it can, in some cases, cause seizures, and that it is not recommended in patients who have suffered a traumatic brain injury.

By the time I realized any of this, I'd pretty much lost my mind.

I remember getting a tattoo at my friend Jim Bob's house, and stopping off at a Walmart on the way home. Don't know why I went there, or what I needed. But I can recall walking through the store, and I remember seeing a display case for one of the *Pirates of the Caribbean* movies that had just been released on DVD. I remember standing there, seeing Johnny Depp's face . . . and then everything went black.

I woke in the emergency room, curled on my side, puking and shitting and pissing all at once. There were doctors and nurses rushing about, yelling at me, screaming.

"Sir! What did you take?!"

"Ughhhh. Nothing."

"What are you on, sir? We need to know what drugs you've taken so we can help."

The room was spinning. My head felt like it was going to explode. I tried to speak but could barely get out a word between retches.

"Nothing . . . I swear."

They ran blood tests, a drug screen, which, of course, came back negative since Tramadol is not a narcotic. I was interviewed by the police. I stayed there for several hours before they let me go. Turns out they'd given me Narcan, which is used to treat people who have overdosed on heroin or other opiates. That's why I'd been so sick—they were purging the system of a presumed drug addict.

I was halfway out the door before I realized that I did not know where I was or how I'd gotten there. I called a couple friends and had them come and pick me up. Days would pass before I tracked down the name of the ambulance company that had brought me to the hospital. They told me that I had been at a Walmart. Slowly . . . things came back to me. A week or more passed before I picked up my car. Predictably, the windows were smashed and some shit had been stolen. I went inside to talk to someone about it. When I introduced myself, the manager nearly started to cry; he looked like he'd seen a ghost.

"Man, I can't believe you're all right."

"Yeah, well . . . barely."

"No, seriously," he said. "You were dead. Our security guard gave you CPR, got you breathing again."

I tried to ask him some questions, but he didn't want to talk about it. The whole incident had clearly left him shaken. He wasn't alone. I had no idea what the fuck was going on with me. Was I dying? If so, I didn't really care. In fact, I welcomed the possibility. My grip on reality was tenuous at best. Paranoia and self-loathing became the fuel in my life. I had this crazy notion that I was at war, and that Brian Deegan was not just someone who had fucked me over in business, but who was now my mortal enemy, and who needed to be exterminated. I'd wake up in weird places with no recollection of how I got there. I had multiple car accidents, sometimes on a single trip. I'd be sitting in my living room, watching television, and all of a sudden I'd start hallucinating—seeing SWAT teams running across my lawn and trying to break into my house. I'd call up my parents and beg for their help.

"Dad, please! Deegan sent them here. They want to kill me!"

I was prone to fits of complete and utter madness. There were times, for example, when I truly thought about killing Brian. Not in the abstract, either, as I had in the past. On more than one occasion, I actually put the plan in motion, going so far as to call him up and try to lure him out into a barren patch of wilderness.

"Hey, Brian," I'd say. "Let's go out and ride tomorrow."

But he was smarter than me, or at least smarter than I gave him credit for being.

"Huh? You haven't called me in three years and now you want to go out for a ride in some place I don't even recognize? No thanks, dude."

I can't say for sure I would have gone through with it. But in my state of mind—depressed, psychotic—it was a distinct possibility. I was in and out of court at the time, running up massive legal bills. I was utterly broke while Brian was driving around in a Bentley, paid for with profits from my business. I hated him for that. And I presumed he hated me. Sometimes I'd hear voices, and I'd imagine they were people hired by Brian to break into my house and slit my throat. More than once I accused my parents of betraying me.

I was delusional.

I was insane.

I started thugging again—not to the level I'd known previously, but enough that it could've gotten me killed or at least thrown in jail. I briefly reentered the world of bareknuckle fighting—this time with the dubious goal of marketing

the videos and making some cash. I didn't care. I figured I didn't deserve anything good that had come into my life anyway. I knew what I was: a piece of
shit; a low-life, scumbag who had lost his mind and would be better off dead.
I'd never just eat a bullet. I wouldn't go out that way. But if I happened to get
killed in the heat of "battle?" Yeah, that was okay. I believed in that shit—the
whole idea of Viking mythology, of striving to reach Valhalla. There was honor
and dignity in a warrior's death. If I went out doing something gnarly on my
bike, well that was okay. If I went out while trying to kill my business partner,
or while thugging on the streets, or simply behind the wheel of my car . . . that
was okay, too.

I just wanted to get to the other side. I wanted the pain to end.

It nearly did.

I was rolling up the Five from San Diego to San Clemente when I blacked
out and lost control of my Dodge pickup. I remember nothing leading up to the
accident, only the bleating of sirens and the voices of paramedics.

"Where is the child?"

I was groggy, disoriented, and for a moment I was filled with panic. Had
Lynkin been in the car with me? Had I killed my son?

No, thank God. I kept a car seat in the truck for those occasions when
Lynkin was with me, and the EMTs had simply seen the seat and presumed the
worst. I was alone. Jesus, was I alone.

An investigation would reveal that I'd probably been traveling in excess of
seventy-five miles per hour when the seizure struck. The car had rolled at least
nine times before coming to a rest on the side of the highway. Somehow I had
avoided striking another vehicle (and likely killing some poor, innocent victim)
along the way. When the paramedics arrived on the scene, I had no pulse—the

seizure, once again, had stopped my heart. A coroner was summoned. By the time he got there, I'd been resuscitated and pulled from the vehicle. Aside from a few bumps and bruises, I was unharmed. The seat belt had saved my life. But for what reason? What purpose?

I got off the Tramadol and started to improve. I started riding again, and surfing. I worked out with a trainer and some guys who were serious about mixed martial arts. I was fit and healthy. And then, in 2008, the weirdest thing began to happen. I started hallucinating again, even though I was completely drug free. I'd wake up in the morning and find that I couldn't get out of bed. Not because I was sad or depressed, but because of deep and painful muscle spasms that essentially rendered me paralyzed. These episodes might last as little as five minutes or as long as an hour. Eventually they'd pass, but they were incredibly scary.

I started hearing voices again. I was gripped by paranoia.

What the fuck is going on? I've never been healthier and I'm still crazy.

My parents took me to Scripps Hospital in La Jolla, where I underwent a battery of physical and psychiatric tests. The conclusion: I was schizophrenic. You could blame the brain injury, the drug use, the excessive amounts of Tramadol I'd poured into my system—some combination of the three, probably. It didn't matter. Physically, they said, there was nothing they could do to help me. I needed long-term psychiatric care and medication.

My parents doubted the diagnosis. They insisted on more tests, more blood work, which eventually showed the strangest thing: traces of chemicals in my blood stream. Arsenic, mercury. The tiniest amounts, but still, enough to wreak havoc on the brain.

Was somebody trying to poison me? Maybe so. As someone with a documented history of paranoia, drug use, and psychotic breaks, I realize that my credibility is somewhat suspect. But there is no denying the forensic evidence; nor the effect on my mind and body. I can think of a few people who would not have shed a tear had I succumbed to rat poison. Of course, I can't prove a thing.

I crawled back to the land of the living in fits and starts—two steps up, one step back. By late 2008, Metal Mulisha had entered into an arrangement with the La Jolla Group, one of the world's premier multi-brand apparel licensing companies. The deal was necessary in order to save the company, which had fallen deep into debt, and was contingent upon a thawing of the ice between Deegan and me. Simply put, we'd have to get along for the sake of Metal Mulisha. I started drawing a salary and hanging out at the office. I became more deeply involved in the running of the business; the closer I looked at our books, the more pissed off I became. In my absence, Metal Mulisha had been run into the ground. I was furious with Brian, and I was disappointed in myself for having ever let it happen.

I started having headaches again. In spite of my disastrous history with the drug, I started taking Tramadol again. The seizures returned almost immediately. I started copping hydro again. And then Valium, which I chewed by the fistful.

Real sobriety came in 2009. It's a cliché, I know, but I got sick and tired of being sick and tired. I despised the lack of control, the feeling that I had no power over my own destiny. Not only that, but the drugs weren't even doing their job any more. I'd built up such a tolerance that I couldn't even get high. I'd just get sick and pass out, sometimes overdosing to the point that I'd wake up on the bathroom floor with my skin turning purple and a drug buddy pounding on my chest.

So one day I just quit. Cold turkey. Holed up in the house and white knuckled it for the better part of a month. Worst pain I've ever known, an unrelenting wave of nausea, chills, and fever. And then it ended. I was clean. But that was only the first step. I had to get rid of my so-called friends, many of whom accused me of being some sort of traitor. This part, as it turned out, was even harder than kicking drugs. I needed help, so I turned to a neighbor who also happened to be a drug counselor. He ran a sober-living recovery center not far from my house.

"Rocky, my problem isn't so much the drugs, because I'm not even using right now," I explained. "It's more a matter of getting away, collecting myself, getting to the root of who I am and what I want out of life."

"No problem," he said. "Why don't you come and stay at my ranch? We'll start with thirty days. If you want to stay for longer, you can stay longer."

And that's what I did. I fell off the face of the Earth for a little while, and when I came back, I began piecing my life together. I started doing positive stuff, helping others. You know, there are people who you want to help, but they can't be helped (I used to be one of those guys, for the longest time). And then there are people who need help, and they want to be helped.

So I started getting those people in and getting them on my program, training and riding with me, helping them stay clean and sober. Helping them change their hateful, hurtful mentality. A kid named Jimmy stayed at my house for a while, riding and working out in my gym while trying to stay sober. He was a budding white supremacist, always thrusting his fist in the air and yelling "White power!" and shit like that, just for effect.

Jimmy was barely twenty years old. It wasn't hard for me to look at him, in his eyes, and see myself a decade earlier and hear the echoes of my voice in his angry, pointless words.

"Jimmy," I'd say. "What the fuck are you doing, man? Look at me. I know who you are. I know your family, remember?"

No bullshit—Jimmy's cousin had been a close friend of mine, before he went to prison over a DUI, and came out ruined, with a swastika tattooed on the top of his head. He went into jail a fairly normal guy and emerged as a killer. Jimmy was heading in the same direction. So I tried to talk some sense into him, make him realize the hypocrisy of his viewpoint, and the senselessness of his rage.

"Look at your own family, dude. Your mom is part Mexican, for Christ's sake. How can you hate these other races when you're intermixed with them?"

He shrugged then sank into himself, like a puppy that had been whacked with a rolled-up newspaper.

I threw an arm around his shoulder.

"Come on, dude. Let's go ride."

It's true what they say—you can't save the world. But if you find a way to get your own shit together, maybe you can help someone else. Small gestures like that did wonders for my soul, and pretty soon I got my fire back. There was no room in my life for chemical substances anymore. There was no room for hate or anger or violence. They had already robbed me of the prime years of my life.

I wouldn't give them another day.

EPILOGUE

December 2012

New York

Check it out . . .

Winter in Brooklyn, and I'm a long way from the sunny skies of California, but feeling right at home with a bunch of guys—kids, really—riding bikes in the streets. I'm out here on business—there's a book to be written and opportunities to expand the Metal Mulisha brand—but this is my passion now. There are kids all over the country (shit, all over the world) who are just like I was—kids who've slipped between the cracks and aren't sure what they're going to do with their lives. Kids who could easily fall into some seriously self-destructive behavior, if they haven't already. For some of them, riding motorcycles is an outlet, a chance to commit to something, to feel good about themselves.

There's scary talent out there in the urban freeriding movement, and I want to do whatever I can to support it. These guys are getting by with virtually nothing but balls and ingenuity; imagine what they could do with the right resources. Think you can't build a freestyle course in Harlem or Brooklyn? Think again. It's going to happen, and if the Metal Mulisha can be part of that, I'll be a happy man.

Come to think of it, I'm already a happy man, blessed in ways too numerous to recount, but let's start with the big one.

I'm still here.

There must be a reason for that. There must be a calling. Look, I don't want to get all preachy; I hated it when people would do that to me, and I'm not going to do it to anyone else. I act primarily now on passion and feeling. I get involved in projects that interest me and lift my spirits, that make me feel good about myself. I'm not an overtly religious man, but there is a spirituality in my life now that previously did not exist. When I was growing up—a lot of religious stuff just didn't make any sense to me. Maybe that's because I wasn't ready for it, or because I was just too angry and fucked up on drugs. For whatever reason, a lot of what I was taught seemed hypocritical and illogical. But I'm trying to give it a second chance.

Hell, I don't know, man. I'm just trying to fit in and do the right thing with whatever time I have left on this planet. I'm trying to help others and be a role model. Not a nag, and not a self-righteous prick. I want to lead by example— by riding well and living clean and acting like a responsible, compassionate adult; by not doing drugs and partying and beating people up. I did enough of that. I can't change my past; I can only try to do better moving forward. I don't expect anyone to share my religious beliefs or be impacted by what I believe. That's a very personal and private matter, and if you find something that works, good for you. I'm a student of the Bible right now, and not a very good one. I'm closer to being a first grader than a PhD candidate. But I do know this: my faith (stange as it might sound, I am studying with the Jehovah's Witnesses) helps put structure in my life; it reminds me that there are lines I cannot cross, lines that separate the man I was from the man I want to be.

Once an addict, always an addict. I know that. I'm not arrogant or stupid enough to think I'll ever win this fight. It goes on and on, ending only when I'm toes-up.

Hopefully, that's a long way off. Too much to live for right now.

I'm really excited about working with Robbie Maddison, the brilliant Australian stunt rider and long-distance jumper, to create new initiatives in free riding and urban riding, to push the envelope of our sport in ways no one has imagined.

And then there's the business, of course. Metal Mulisha came back virtually from the dead in the last couple years—morphing from a company that was bleeding red ink into one that had more than $30 million in sales in 2011. Our licensing arrangement with the La Jolla Group certainly helped pump new life into the company, but I'd also like to think that I've had a lot to do with it. I've been something of a silent partner—Brian Deegan remains the public face of the Mulisha—but I know what I've done behind the scenes. I know that I've helped turn things around, and that my motives remain pure. I've had opportunities to sell my share of the company. I could have made millions and walked away, but I haven't done that, and I won't do that, because if I go, there will be no one left to fight for the riders who wear the Mulisha logo. It's never been about the money for me, and it never will be. For the time being, an uneasy truce exists between Brian and me, but who knows what the future holds. I'll do what I have to do in order to protect the company I founded, and to protect the people who depend on that company. In fact, I am currently in the process of trying to buy out Brian's share of Metal Mulisha. We'll see what the future holds.

A bunch of us live in the same neighborhood now, world-class freeriders devoted to pushing the limits of the sport, and to developing young talent. We share a huge training and riding compound known as the MDP Block that's open to anyone with the right attitude. Not long ago we put on a demonstration for more than thirty at-risk youth from San Diego's Outdoor Outreach program. These were kids who'd been dealt a tough hand in life—tougher than I was dealt, to be honest; at least I had parents who loved me. I want kids like that to understand that there is a place for them, and that there are options. I'll open my freestyle track to these kids; I'll open my home to them.

There is one little guy who shows tremendous promise—both on and off the track. They call him Wombat Jr. or Little Wombat. He's ten years old, loves motocross, skateboarding, and photography—can already do shit with Adobe Photoshop that blows my mind!

I'm making up for lost time with Lynkin. His mom ran into some problems a while back, and I've had full legal custody for more than a year and a half now. I can't really put into words what he means to me. Lynkin is my son and my best friend; he is my partner and my purpose. We are virtually inseparable. I am trying to raise him in an atmosphere of love and trust and openness, but with a firm hand, as well. Kids need structure and guidance and consistency; they need to know you will always be there for them, and that the world isn't quite as scary a place as it sometimes seems to be. They need to know that you care.

I don't keep a lot of secrets from Lynkin. He knows I was absent for years. He knows I am a recovering drug addict. He knows, in abstract terms, at least, that I did some bad things. I don't try to hide any of that from him, or pretend that it didn't happen. Sometimes I think kids are so sheltered and kept on such a short leash that when you give them a little slack, they never stop running.

A little knowledge can be a good thing in the struggle to lead a healthy life. My son understands that there are good decisions and bad decisions, and that there are consequences to actions. Obviously I don't want to expose my ten-year-old son to drugs and sex and alcohol, but the fact is, that's the world we live in. I'm not going to act like it's not there. I'm going to educate him and talk with him, and do everything I can to keep the lines of communication open. I have no shortage of friends who have lost everything—including their lives—because of drugs, and I don't mind pointing that out to Lynkin.

He's a smart kid; he'll figure it out. And I'll be with him every step of the way.

In the meantime, I want him to be proud of me—for the way I ride and the work that I do. I sit there sometimes and imagine Lynkin coming home from school crying because some kid has said something mean to him: *"Yeah, I know your dad—he's a fuckin' drug addict."* Nah, I can't let that happen. That possibility alone is enough to get me out on the bike; it keeps me honest and grounded.

I'm riding well these days, too. I'm as healthy and fit as I've been since . . . well . . . maybe ever. I've been doing a lot of surfing, chasing big waves with Nathan Fletcher. But the best days are when I'm out there in the backyard with Lynkin, following him around the track, watching him ride and seeing his long blond hair flowing beneath his helmet, and flashing that smile when he hits a jump perfectly.

That's my boy, and I'll be there for him, whether he nails a landing or falls flat on his face and needs someone to pick him up and dust him off; someone to give him a hug and tell him everything will be all right.

I'm not going anywhere.